Get out of your mind jail

Get out of mind jail

BY REVEREND NICHOLAS BARRETT

NEW YORK

Tribute

To my mother and father,

Your graceful life and your living memory are in the golden
stream of eternity, which inspired and finally unlocked
the hidden dimensions of my life.

Get Out of Mind Jail
Create Your New Life With Purpose

Published in New York, New York, by Morgan James Publishing. Morgan James and The Entrepreneurial Publisher are trademarks of Morgan James, LLC. www.MorganJamesPublishing.com

The Morgan James Speakers Group can bring authors to your live event. For more information or to book an event visit The Morgan James Speakers Group at www.TheMorganJamesSpeakersGroup.com.

9781630478711   paperback
9781630478728   eBook
9781630478735   casebound

Library of Congress Control Number: 2015918260

Shelfie

A **free** eBook edition is available with the purchase of this print book.

CLEARLY PRINT YOUR NAME ABOVE IN UPPER CASE

Instructions to claim your free eBook edition:
1. Download the Shelfie app for Android or iOS
2. Write your name in **UPPER CASE** above
3. Use the Shelfie app to submit a photo
4. Download your eBook to any device

Cover Design by:
John Weber

Interior Design by:
Brittany Bondar

In an effort to support local communities, raise awareness and funds, Morgan James Publishing donates a percentage of all book sales for the life of each book to Habitat for Humanity Peninsula and Greater Williamsburg.

Get involved today! Visit
www.MorganJamesBuilds.com

Habitat for Humanity®
Peninsula and Greater Williamsburg
Building Partner

Contents

Preface

Get out of Mind Jail is a book birthed out of the depths of my heart. It was revealed to me that the societal values I had taken on, which may be similar to yours, were lies I had accepted as truths. I'd been on a quest seeking value from sources outside myself, so I could be thought of as whole and accepted.

The craving for purpose and meaning for our individual lives is not in personal achievements, fame or fortune. From the beginning of times people have achieved and attained all of these things, and indeed ended up more needy than before. This search can only be resolved when a person is willing to open the depths of his or her soul. The answer has been in existence since the beginning of time. We must swim beyond the shoreline, plunge deep within ourselves, and search patiently, diligently, until the answer emerges.

The answer is in God, the One, who from nothing created everything, the alpha and omega, the living water— labels for what we, in our technological age, would call transformation. Transformation means radical change of form, the way a caterpillar turns into a butterfly. In human terms, the metamorphosis would be a shift, a change of character, taking on a new likeness, renewing the mind and spirit. This means allowing anger, doubts, and hostility to become peace, empathy, and love. One divine moment of revelation can set a person on a whole new course, and a new life.

Is this possible in our innate human nature? What we know by what is evident in a present day world: the external realms of money, prestige, education, or anything we attach ourselves to can offer only illusion, and at best some temporal solution. It's the inner Being that brings lasting change and endures regardless of what's on the outside. The inner Being craves meaning and purpose. But where do we find meaning, and what is our purpose? A life spent on the surface will never answer these questions or satisfy the needs that challenge us to seek them.

It is a cultural myth, one I used to believe, that technology helps us find answers. But if that were the case, then surely in our age the soul's questions should have been addressed. Today we outsmart our own ecosystem, manipulating soil to produce rainfall-like effects, creating penguin robots that walk the ocean floor. Yet the questions of our inner Being have only grown more urgent. With all this knowledge, you and I know less about the purpose of life than our ancestors.

We live in the age of the computer and sophisticated learning. Over the past few generations, the cerebral cortex has developed significantly, far surpassing the boundaries of any time before. But the cortex, often referred to as the new brain, does not give us the ability to feel and be. All living things possess this capacity, including the human inhabitants of this planet, but in us it is diminished. We have become alienated in our own world. We have lost touch with all we were created to be and have taken on a false self.

You are perfectly made with a unique plan and purpose for your life, with everything you need already mapped out and available to complete your life successfully. You may see yourself in different terms because societal patterns encourage you to view yourself through labels. These can include successful, unsuccessful, rich, poor, slim, overweight, accepted, or not accepted, judged by the job you do. Bound by these norms, you are a spectator in life, waiting for some new solution to bring you what you need.

When you live in truth, life flows with revelation, smoothly and purposefully. You stop striving and struggling to get things you feel you need. You see more of all that is already great, all around you, and find that most answers have already been revealed.

In simple terms it comes down to living in a separated, individualistic state, or a life connected to God (Source). The former is a life bent on struggle and isolation, the latter one with purpose, meaning and surety. This can afford you separation or unity. You are a sensory person who smells, hears, feels, sees. Unity intertwines these modes into a single manifestation. One doesn't take away from the other because they all exist as part of one body created in God's image. (Cited en.m.wikipedia.org)

The tragedy is not that we die but that we take so long to start living. Our experiences create an imprint from the moment we leave the womb and begin listening to the words of our parents, classmates, and the media. Too often they offer us disappointment, heartbreak, letdown, which we then edit into our perceptions. This leaves us in a perpetual state of looking at the present through the mirror of the past, our "mind jail." I sometimes refer to this as Human Mind TiVo, where the prison of presumptive thinking lies.

My constant observation of human behavior and study of the human mind have compelled me to share this book with you. After coming out of the dark and into the light myself, I understand the darkness most of us live our entire lives in. If I had not been there before, I wouldn't have known the disappointment, misery, and fear it causes and how it can be the catalyst for us to spend our days in negative contemplation, where we prepare for what may or may not happen rather than enjoy the present moment. If we never become aware of our patterns, we risk spending our lives in a stressful state, which becomes like paying interest on a debt we do not owe.

The noise of our mind and the society that influences it keep us behind a veil that obscures the real self. You need to lift the veil and reveal the real you.

Therefore, this book must elucidate on two fronts. First, it must inspire you that there really is an answer—a Master Plan and purpose for your life. Second, it must ignite you to feel the passion and motivation required to live that purpose. This isn't something you can put on hold until you find the right time. You had this plan and purpose before you were knitted in your mother's womb and have been ready to discover the journey that was planned for you. Sadly, most of us dismiss hundreds of experiences that could make transformation a reality. If it weren't for the enormous effort we put into denial, repression, and doubt, each life would be a constant revelation.

Ultimately, the defining point to discovering the real self is believing your life is worth exploring with passion and conviction. I don't expect to change human nature with this book, though I do hope to uplift the consciousness of those who may read it, showing why many think the way they do. These revelations changed my own life into something bigger, as my daily self became refreshed, light, and joyous—one who looks forward to each new day with zest, as opposed to the struggle I used to feel.

I want the best for your life, too, as I am certain you do. When you explore this book, my hope is that you will be restored with the turning of every page, as you go deeper into unraveling yourself and taking steps toward a new way of living. We only have this day, so why not use it to mark the beginning of the rest of your life? Why not live a life that frees you from labels and the bondage of self-imposed limitation and suffering? You can have the life God made uniquely for you.

You have suffered enough! Even at this moment, the suffering emerges from within you as you hold this book in your hands and read these syllables that speak of the possibility of living a full and joyous life. In this new life, you no longer inflict sadness on yourself or others through the negative thinking of the past or the false limitations you've placed on your joy. You no longer base what's coming in the future on what has already happened.

My intent is for you to use this human-mind manual as an introduction to a new life. As the advice contained here changed my life from the inside out, I hope that it will also change yours. Thank you for allowing me the opportunity to try. Thanks foremost to God for teaching me the light and wisdom to share with you amazing people.

Blessings,

Reverend Nicholas Barrett

Introduction

I want to briefly tell you how I came to the place of writing this book. For more than a decade, I was blessed to work with professional athletes to maximize their fitness and performance through my expertise in various exercise modals, clinical nutrition, and supplementation. I had been trapped in this false reality and limitation that I am what I do. This is like a badge we wear to attach to an identity and purpose for being here. This is an illusion and prison I lived with until I was older than 30. Today I feel like I am talking about someone else's life, as I have taken on a whole new form and function.

I don't dwell in the past, however, I feel it important to inform of the journey that led me to become an author and empowerment speaker. It was on a certain trip to London in 2006 to visit my parents for the Christmas period that I noticed my father, a usually athletic, handsome man, looking weak and ashen. My mother informed me that he had Parkinson's disease and had a limited time to live. On hearing this, my mind took on a new reality of our transiency, and this precious gift that another day gives us with each fingerprinted sunrise and sunset. How often we fall short of recognizing its peerless glory in our limited peripheral vision. I visited from Los Angeles on many occasions for the next two years, during which I kept in daily communication. It was on my trip in 2008 that I returned to my father's wake. I recall the day as vividly today as on the morning of December 19, 2008, when I walked through a long chamber-like room to witness my hero lying in rest, clothed in his pinstriped suit. It was made even more poignant as it was my mother's birthday. My heart was shattered into a thousand pieces, as if shards of glass were scattered across the floor of the earth's surface. As I looked down at his face, which had a smiling, heavenly caressed presence, I found myself in the corridor of many doors, some leading to nowhere and some to divine purpose for my life. It was like an awakening of the senses that I had not previously experienced. I was engulfed in golden rays of light, transcending time of feeling. I felt the presence of God like never before. His invitation that you can either continue to do this alone or come on board and live your life not to gather for self, but to give strength and encouragement to others.

I had a strange feeling of being outside of the previous confines of my body. It was as if I were free from being trapped and restrained by worry and time. My mind was aware, but it was as if God had put His arm on my shoulder and said "fear not, as I will always be with you, I am your Father." My heart felt the presence of God as all the incessant worry, anxiety, and mind-chatter had ceased. It was if a deep void had been replaced and filled with an awesome calm. It's like my knees touched the floor, at the same rising to heaven. I realized that we are limited in our separation and hold onto our body, while it is merely a container to a timeless, straight line into eternity. I was fully at peace and gripped by a powerful reality.

As I exited the room to join my mother and brother who had been waiting while I paid my last respects, there remained a still calm in me, a feeling of a new inner strength and awareness I had not previously known. As we left the building I looked up at the sky, the birds and flora all around me. I noticed the sky as if a blanket of azure magnificence, the birds chirping and their colors and outlines as if a precious gem, indeed everything had a powerful presence of grace and uniqueness in its miracle of creation. This was like a priceless gift. It became apparent that this was my transporter for consciousness. Praise God for all His wonderful works.

Not too dissimilar to the way a caterpillar becomes a butterfly, if we also permit change to take place, we can ignite a metamorphosis that can bring with it a whole new way of life. The change science cannot even explain goes on as a mystery on the inside and then manifests itself on the outside. This change has always been a potential that we have carried with us, and then becomes activated by life's challenges and circumstances. We try to run from God, but the reality is that He will get you whether willing or by circumstance, and this is an amazing awakening to the human soul.

It is within using my passion for learning about what empowers people, my study of the human mind and psychology, with observation of people and their behaviors, that I have moved into my true purpose to illuminate the human consciousness. Through my conviction to improve myself as a person, I now answer to a greater calling to help others have a lighter, brighter, more flourishing existence. It is only when we can make others greater first that we become greater ourselves. This, for me, is the ultimate paradox as we kneel down to bring others up, only ultimately to be brought up ourselves. Glory to God.

The mind is the vital component that holds it all together, as it's important to never build a castle on just sand, which may be vast but will crumble in time due to its weak foundation. The more we focus on developing our minds by renewing them with positive thoughts, the more abundance we let into our lives—and the more able we are to tap into our true potential. Then it becomes easier to live the life we want to live, not one that our mind restricts us to living. Many of us think that something big needs to happen to change our lives, as we overlook the small altogether, though it is actually the small that can become the big. A single decision could be thought of as small, but it can make all the difference in the outcome of someone's life.

Most of us spend our days making decisions based upon our past experiences. We all have cells in our bodies that store and then transfer information—the human equivalent of TiVo for the mind. The moment we come out of the womb, we're all the same, with no past experiences or interactions with the outside world. Then our experiences, whether from parents, schoolmates, colleagues, etc. begin to leave an imprint in our minds and the cells throughout our entire bodies. So, instead of living in the present moment, we are too often living out of an edit from the imprint we have created from our past. We absorb things like a sponge and are mostly unaware of how we limit our lives through our thought patterns and learned behaviors that are stored deep within our subconscious minds. If these are not recognized and redirected, we could under-live our entire lives as a result of this subconscious nemesis. This can become a limiting belief that puts a cap on our true potential. It is only when we gain this awareness that we can make our minds right. This means we need to adjust our attitudes and interpretations of our present circumstances so we can live full lives.

Let's look at an example. We may say something like, "The traffic on the freeway is going to be really heavy tomorrow" or "There's going to be fog on the drive." We're always preparing for the worst scenario. People rarely say, "The traffic is going to be light on the freeway" or "There's going to be a beautiful blue sky during the drive." Instead, we're always focused on the bad. This has a lot to do with the interactions we witness within our families during childhood. Most people, due to their exposure to negative responses and behaviors from their childhood, are conditioned to be negative. Unless we develop an awareness of this thought pattern, we will stay in a state of our subconscious mind micromanaging our conscious mind, in a way that is always preparing us for a negative experience.

All the things we observe are channeled through a filter and, until we work consistently on redirecting our thought patterns—which are mostly cyclical and triggered by various stimuli from either our perceptions of what may happen or learned behaviors that are designed to protect us from challenging situations—we will remain in a holding pattern. The fact is that these behaviors put limits on our days and potential, which is what makes them a "mind jail." It is the dark that surrounds humanity in our fallen world. If we focus on the negative news in the world's media, our minds will dwell on the negative and remain unconditioned for the positive to happen. Our minds are mirrors of what our eyes see and our ears hear.

So what happens when we are not enlightened or aware? Look at it this way: All of us have a percentage of darkness in our bodies. These are the negative things stored from our heartbreaks, traumas, and disappointments. Obviously, the more darkness we have, the more negative cells we've stored and the more TiVo we have in our memory banks. That memory bank impacts our lives by keeping us making decisions based on the things that have happened in our pasts.

If we minimize our darkness, we'll get much more out of our lives. Only then can we pull ourselves out of a mind jail of our own making and become open to all that is available to us. The world is very spacious, and if we keep our minds in a box, this will dictate the amount of space we ultimately have. Everything boils down to how we perceive our days and interpret our immediate circumstances. Our interpretation of events is really what our day becomes, and ultimately what our lives become. A day will only be as good as our interpretation of it. All days are great, but are we going to raise our perceptions to meet their greatness? Raising perception is the ability to perceive, to feel, or to be conscious of events, objects, thoughts, emotions, or sensory patterns. In this level of consciousness, sense data can be confirmed by an observer without necessarily implying understanding, getting into a point of feeling good intrinsically, and then not relying on outcomes or circumstances to dictate feelings. When we do this, we get into a state of feeling much lighter and more positive about life, and we radiate a renewed energy that attracts the same. In simplest terms, what we put out is what comes back. (Cited sermoncity.powerserve.net)

The things that are going to happen are going to happen regardless, but the way we interpret them is going to determine whether we live a calm life of abundance, rooted in the present, or a life that's jaded and not open to good things happening. To make a change, we have to identify where we are today and then consistently work on changing the way we think about life. We need to focus less on the dissatisfaction we have and turn toward the abundance so we may, in turn, attract more of it. Abundance is found in being comfortable within our own circumstances through putting the focus on what we have, making it visible and letting it attract more.

Let's take another example: Imagine a guy who lives in a house on a steep hill. One day, his tire goes flat and his wife asks him how they will get the tire changed. The man says, "The neighbor is home, I know he's got a jack, but he's not a nice guy. I'm going to get up there and he's going to chew me out. He won't be interested in helping me." So the guy walks up the hill, all the while anticipating how unhelpful his neighbor will be. By the time his neighbor opens the door, the man says, "Well, I don't think you can help me; I've got my car at the bottom of the hill with a flat tire." The neighbor says, "Hey, that's OK. Don't worry, I'm here for you." The two go to the car and change the tire together. At the end of the day, the guy sits back in his car and says to his wife, "Oh, wow, that's unbelievable. The neighbor was so generous and willing to help me." In this sense, his mind wasn't allowing him to prepare for a positive outcome—it was in mind jail. He wasn't in a place of being open and ready to accept that good things could happen. How many of you are living your lives like this today?

This applies to so many situations in life today, even in ways we may not be aware of. It could relate to preparing for a job interview, a medical exam, a vacation, or a new relationship. A self-contained reality can become our whole world for the rest of our lives unless we make changes. It's important to coach the mind as it's like a muscle, which, if untrained, will grow weak and underproductive. If we want to live our lives to their fullest potential, we must train the mind with consistency so that we can change our lives forever. The more we refocus the mind by renewing our thought patterns, the more abundance we'll find within our lives and the easier it will be to live the lives we want to live, not the ones our minds restrict us to.

Of course, there will be times when things will not go smoothly. However, when we put our focus on believing that all things are working together for our benefit, it is amazing how life can change. Like attracts like, so having a positive attitude and a good perspective will bring more joy and goodness to us. In short, a better quality of life. A negative mind-set can create health issues, as stress is the number one killer. Heart disease, blood pressure, and stroke, to a large degree, are all triggered by stress. Many people are taking medications for chronic conditions, and this is why people are sicker than at any time before. The pharmaceutical industry is more profitable because we're encouraging people to take pharmaceuticals to combat some of the effects of stress, even as we already have the answer in our hands—that changing our interpretation of things will help cure us. We have turned into a population of highly stressed, mostly unfulfilled, discontented, self-obsessed, angry people who are not aware of how our learned thought patterns and behaviors are impacting our health and, by extension, our lives.

In a 2010 report by the Centers for Disease Control, a survey conducted from 1999 to 2008 checked the blood pressure of more than 24,000 adults and found that, during that period, the percentage of adults aware they had high blood pressure increased to nearly 81 percent, up from 70 percent. Also, nearly 74 percent were taking medicine to control their blood pressure, up from about 60 percent. About a quarter of Americans had high blood pressure in the early 1990s. By the end of that decade, that figure had reached 30 percent. The latest figures indicate that about 74 million people are impacted by high blood pressure. (Cited severehypertension.net)

It's important to remember that our minds will flow in any direction we choose to take them. The mind is akin to a drainage system in a house. Imagine such a system at the end of fall, when leaves are coming down and blocking up certain areas. There's no free flow, things get jammed, and when it rains there are leaks. Similarly, when things get blocked in our minds, they prevent anything that comes along from flowing, which keeps us trapped.

But we can transcend this and do away with the things that we've stored. "This person is working against me," "It'll be crowded," "I'll be competing for space"—these statements are the ego in control."

The smoothness we have in our lives is the smoothness we've created. Life doesn't create itself, we need to create it. We can control the direction of our lives by the decisions and choices we make rather than allowing stress to control us. Stress will be forever present as a human condition; however, it is in how we handle it that can put us in either a mind jail or challenge us to live a better life. If we allow it, our minds can set a limit on our lives and our abilities, putting us on cruise control. When we change our human mind GPS and reprogram our cruise control, we do not change the destination, as that's mapped out already, we simply change our journey because of the new way we interpret and perceive the things in front of us. The intangible challenges and circumstances of life that come up will not go away, but we'll see them as hurdles to jump over and not walls to crash into. Challenges will instead become opportunities to improve and help us appreciate life more.

The great thing is that mind-sets can be transformed, so in the same way that your life is caught up in a learned way of thinking today, a whole new way of thinking could be upon you tomorrow. You can transform your life from one of chains and struggles to one of contentment, joy, and peace. We all have this one life to live, so why settle for any less? The story will never stop, although one day we will no longer play a part. We can live our whole lives trying to control it, but it's in the letting go that the real journey can begin to find the real purpose for being here.

My prayer is that you enjoy this journey of shared wisdom and give all the thanks to Him.

CHAPTER ONE

Negative Mind TiVo in Relationships

If you have a "resonance," which I am certain that you do as a human, this would mean you have stored negative cells, due to past hurtful experiences or disappointments. These may have taken shape from a number of things. This can be from being called hurtful names, failed relationships, career disappointments, or anything else that has not met your expectations. Chances are that each of us has experienced at least one, if not all of these things at some point in our lives. Negative pain resonances are often stimulated by events in our most intimate relationships, known as triggers.

Relationships present a great opportunity for developing awareness of our reactions to situations and a unique opportunity to become aware of and ultimately conquer our past pain nemeses. Humans especially exhibit the most extreme manifestation of negative mind resonance within personal relationships.

Every emotional situation we encounter leaves behind an impression. The type of impression it leaves is based on our own interpretation of the event, which, if perceived as negative, is manifested as pain. This pain becomes stored in our bodies and acts as negative energy, representing a certain "darkness" in an individual. In differing degrees, it may be harbored in an active or inactive memory bank. The active bank involves more recent pain, such as enduring a challenging season of life. Inactive banks involve childhood hurts, which can leave deep residual scars.

The amount of darkness can vary from 10 percent in more aware and enlightened individuals to 90 percent or even 100 percent in those individuals who are most negative and depressed. The greater the degree of stored pain, the more an individual reacts to present situations through the stored pain of the past.

Triggers that cause us to react to a situation can be activated at any time without warning. The place where individuals feel most free to unleash the darkness of their full-blown pain body is in the most unlikely place: their closest personal relationships. The very place where one would expect to find love and harmony can sometimes end up providing target practice for abuse and the venting of unresolved pain. As an example, a couple could be taking a drive when one of them makes what he or she feels to be an innocent observation, which causes the other to explode in a rage, leaving the other person puzzled. Another way a person can react is to withdraw from the relationship, which is an attempt to punish the other in a passive-aggressive way. Another example is when a person leaves a voicemail for a friend suggesting they meet for coffee the following morning, subject to confirmation on that morning. If the friend shows up to the café assuming that the other person will be there and finds himself alone, he may react in anger and subsequently withdraw his friendship in a way that punishes the friend for the slight. The person is made to feel diminished, unloved, or unimportant in some way in this otherwise innocent situation based on something that happened in his past. These feelings, in most cases, stem from some kind of abandonment issue or lack of attention from one or both parents during childhood, which may make the person extra sensitive when these events reoccur. This leaves a void that, if not worked out, can haunt a person for the rest of his life.

When you are hoping to find a partner, you want to take your time in making certain you determine the person's emotional well-being and how he or she reacts to challenges and everyday life stressors. The common denominator is that the way our own unique negative mind resonance reacts is the same way as another person's, with the only difference being the level of hurt and emotional pain it has stored. When the negative resonance becomes active, it seeks only one thing: more pain. It seeks either to attack the other person, attack itself, or sometimes attack both. Generally speaking, once the negative resonance is activated, it will not stop until it feels replenished with pain. Like anything else, pain bodies need fuel to survive, as this is the only way the subconscious can continue to control our conscious.

It is only through consistent, applied effort that a person can become aware of his or her reactions in the subconscious, which can be turned into one's conscious, and thus lead to healing through awareness. When the pain body is still present and unresolved, it can become activated without any prior notice. To resolve the problems associated with the pain body, we must first gain an awareness of how we feel before these reactive behaviors begin, and examine what circumstances occur before an attack or outburst is triggered. Oftentimes, it is when we are tired and stressed from the routine of a long day, when the challenges of work, finances, commuting, or personal relationships can aggravate us. The more tired we become, the more irritated we can be. As the adage goes, misery loves company.

Being aware of ourselves in all situations, particularly when we feel extra sensitive and likely to explode, is a tool that can minimize the likelihood of our negative mind resonance from having dominating influence over our minds and actions. Developing this awareness is key in moving away from those reactions. After a pain body attack, we are always sorry about what we've done or said because we return to our rational state, from which can see our behavior more clearly. However, we think we have little to do with our negative resonance, which can be completely separate entities within the same person.

In a close relationship, the dormant negative resonance loves its partner and is thankful for the person. When activated, however, it seeks to hurt or destroy, while also seeking to hurt itself. In these cases, neither of the two sides may appear to have any awareness of the other. When a person's negative mind resonance is in the active state, it has no thoughts, emotions, or rationality. The person is in an emotional state and the mind looks to attach itself to another to maintain its force. This may cause the formation of a codependent relationship. This type of relationship is one in which one person depends on a partner for something that is lacking within him or herself.

When we adopt a mind-set of greater awareness, however, we increase our possibility of maximizing our lives by positively impacting our present circumstances. We can do this by becoming more aware of our moods and emotions, as this enables us to become more aware of our triggers, which limits the power of our negative mind.

Working on being fully aware of our present is a very powerful tool to combating this inner saboteur. To help achieve this I exercise at the gym or take a power walk outdoors. During my walk, I get out of my mind while becoming aware of all that's around me. Everything becomes very clear, bright, and spacious. By doing some kind of recreational activity, we can clear our minds and move away from negative mind chatter. As with any other habit or learned way of thinking, we need to practice diverting our thoughts on a regular basis. By working this new way of thinking into our daily, weekly and monthly routines, it will eventually become the subconscious way we think and live, just as real as the way we think and live today.

Becoming aware of the silence and stillness around us also helps us connect to the calmness around our emotions. This state of awareness can become a great tool for diminishing the pain body and keeping our reactions rooted in the present. That way, we can control them rather than allowing them to control us.

Another way of managing our pain body is to become aware of when our thoughts turn toward blaming friends or thinking of ways to hurt them, or when we have thoughts focused on justifying our actions or being seen as right. When we recognize that our attitude has assumed any of these elements, we're beginning to operate with our pain body instead of our rational selves.

Humans are known to have about 50 thoughts every minute, with the negative thoughts outweighing the positive by 14 to 1. We need only to turn on the radio or evening news to be besieged with negative reporting, so it's no wonder that we are more prone to being negative. It's only through greater awareness that we can get our heads right and reconfigure the way we have been conditioned to think. The way forward is to find out what triggers us, work through those triggers by developing our awareness of when they become present, and consistently practice this until they become diminished. Like anything else in life, you have to get over it to get through it.

In communication with another person, whether on the telephone, or in person, slow your mind down and put the focus on the other person's voice, and not what is going on all around. Take deep breaths, as this will help slow down your inner mind chatter. As the mind always wants to respond as it has been conditioned by society, you will now be in a position to listen to what the other person is saying as opposed to merely trying to get your thoughts out. While we have too many thoughts, it will always present a challenge when trying to focus on what someone else is saying. It is when we are more present that we can start to listen, and most importantly, hear the other person. This is the very essence of how we were created to be, at one with each other, created in God's loving image. When we really think about it, how can we love if all we hear are our thoughts within our agenda? It is by separating thoughts that we can develop unity with all others who we encounter.

Next time you are out in a café or restaurant, listen and observe groups of people in conversation. It will become very apparent after a while that most people are not fully hearing the other person/people, but are merely bent on getting their five cents out. We become caught up in our own monologue, solitary, isolated, and alone in a crowd. In this tug of war within our minds, it will always be a challenge to have deep or meaningful relationships. By practicing being out of our minds, our relationships can flourish to new realms and depths not experienced before. Learn to communicate not to the person but with the person. Thinking things through before speaking is better than talking at the person. Most people have said something that they have then lived on to regret in a relationship. Worse still, you could be saying something detrimental and not realizing it. By thinking before you speak, you become more effective and develop better relationships.

As human beings, it's not possible to be with someone many years and always say the "right thing." However, an awareness makes it more likely to say fewer "wrong things." If you compare a relationship to a bank account, negative things are withdrawals and positive things deposits. There is evidence that more successful relationships have a higher level of deposits to withdrawals in the way that they talk to each other. One thing is certain: The negative things said stick much longer than the positive.

Love/Hate Relationships

Unless a relationship begins on a platonic level and can remain in the parallels of giving and not getting, it will be like most relationships, and particularly sexual relationships, deeply flawed and ultimately dysfunctional. The couple may start out great for a while, when they are in the "in love" stage, as they are hormonal due to the sexual newness of each other. Invariably after about the three- to six-month period, "that apparent perfection gets disrupted, as arguments, conflicts, dissatisfaction, and emotional or even physical violence occur with increasing frequency. It seems that most romantic relationships become love/hate relationships before long." Love can then turn into savage attack, feelings of hostility, or complete withdrawal of affection at the flick of a switch. This is considered normal. The relationship then oscillates for a while, a few months or a few years, between the polarities of "love" and hate, and it gives you as much pleasure as it gives you pain. It is not uncommon for couples to become addicted to those cycles. Their drama makes them feel alive. When a balance between the positive/ negative polarities is lost and the negative, destructive cycles occur with increasing frequency and intensity, which tends to happen sooner or later, then it will not be long before the relationship finally collapses." (Cited yourpagemaker.com)

As most relationships are founded on one person needing the other, they are maintained by a destructive cycle of negative and positive coexisting in perpetuity. It is this codependency that prevents the interdependency necessary to maintain and sustain a healthy relationship. The positive already contains within itself the as-yet manifested negative. Both are in fact different aspects of the same dysfunction. I am speaking here of modern day relationships that often become sexual on the third date, as this is commonly referred to as the "sex date." True love has no opposite, as it is built on bringing a whole person to the table, as opposed to fulfilling of a need. This is not mind-based but heart-based. Unconditional love on an ongoing basis is very rare—as rare as enlightened people. There can be periods of love, even in dysfunctional relationships; however, it is sporadic at best.

"The negative side of a relationship is, of course, more easily recognizable as dysfunctional than the positive one. And it is also easier to recognize the source of negativity in your partner than to see it in yourself. It can manifest in many forms: possessiveness, jealousy, control, withdrawal, and unspoken resentment; the need to be right, insensitivity, and self-absorption; emotional demands and manipulation; the urge to argue, criticize, judge, blame, or attack; anger, unconscious revenge for past pain inflicted by a parent, rage, and physical violence." (Cited nonduality.com)

The setup is the feeling of being "in-love," and the newness of the body and sexual euphoria that leaves you feeling deeply satisfied, on the surface. This is predicated by the illusion that you feel loved, your partner wants you more than anyone before, and this gives you a euphoric feeling of joyousness and value. What sustains it is that the other person feels exactly the same. In the company of the person, you feel complete. The feelings can become so intense that the relationship becomes your whole life and nothing else matters. However, you may also have noticed that there is a neediness and a clinging quality to that intensity. You become addicted to the other person. He or she acts like an antidepressant drug on you. You are on a high when the drug is available, but even the possibility or the thought that he or she might no longer be there for you can lead to jealousy, possessiveness, attempts at manipulation through emotional blackmail, blaming, and accusing—fear of loss. If the other person does leave you, this can give rise to the most intense hostility or the most profound grief and despair. In an instant, loving tenderness can turn into a vengeful attack or desperate grief. Where is the love now? Can love change into its opposite in an instant? Was it love in the first place, just filling a need, or a feeling that became addictive? (Cited uros75.blogspot.com)

How Can the Love Last?

The relationship needs to be built on a foundation of solid principle between two whole people becoming one. This takes the time to nurture and grow a friendship that is not built on lust, but on mutual respect. When it happens fast, it ends fast, or is sustained by fulfilling a lack or an unhealthy need. Don't get fooled by the veil of falseness, but instead stay calm and get to know the person, his or her heart, and not his or her body. Remember that societal norms are not working, as is made apparent by a 5.3 in 10 divorce rate in the US in 2014. Make your primary motivation to bring something to the other person, and not the norm of simply taking. In keeping within this fundamental sentiment, you will not only be building up the other person, but building yourself up too.

Marriage is not the institution of man. God instituted marriage, by it being His Plan, that man and woman come together to form the unit of humanity.

Genesis 2:18–25 The Message (MSG) (Cited biblegateway.com)

18–20 God said, "It's not good for the Man to be alone; I'll make him a helper, a companion." So God formed from the dirt of the ground all the animals of the field and all the birds of the air. He brought them to the Man to see what he would name them. Whatever the Man called each living creature, that was its name. The Man named the cattle, named the birds of the air, named the wild animals; but he didn't find a suitable companion.

21–22, God put the Man into a deep sleep. As he slept he removed one of his ribs and replaced it with flesh. God then used the rib that he had taken from the Man to make

Woman and presented her to the Man.

23–25, The Man said, "Finally! Bone of my bone, flesh of my flesh! Name her Woman for she was made from Man." Therefore a man leaves his father and mother and embraces his wife. They become one flesh. The two of them, the Man and his Wife, were naked, but they felt no shame.

How Can I Put This into My Life?

Let's start with affirmations, as these bring with them the assertion of a condition that is already in you. This is powerful, as it brings the revelation of a new truth, which predicates a whole new way of intentionally looking at yourself to bring about powerful transformative qualities to your external environment.

Affirmations: My purpose is to serve. My purpose is to love. I am here to be the change I need to see through being it myself. I am here to live as my true self. I am here to improve and add value to the world I live in.

Relationally: I will appreciate someone not based upon his or her response. I will be empathetic and patient. I will be loving to a person who has shown negative energy toward me. I will take ownership of one situation that has made me feel responsible.

Raising my Presence: I will spend the conversation putting emphasis on observing instead of speaking. I will sit in a quiet place to get in touch with my inner self and my emotions. If someone frustrates or angers me, I will ask myself what I really feel beneath the anger—and I want to work through that feeling until it subsides.

Acceptance: I will spend five minutes thinking about the best qualities of someone I have an issue with. I will think of something a person I know is doing that I don't agree with, and then put myself in his or her set of circumstances to get a better idea of what he or she might be feeling. I will look in the mirror and describe myself exactly as if I were judging myself the way I would like to see myself. Focus on what God says, "I am fearfully and wonderfully made," "I am created in His image," "I am a masterpiece created for a time just like this."

Dos and Don'ts

Dos:

- Express how YOU feel.
- Say how much you appreciate the person.
- Increase positive thoughts and words.
- Take responsibility.
- Think before you speak.

Don'ts:

- Avoud silence (being passive-aggressive).
- Tell someone you want him or her to change.
- Reduce sarcasm.
- Don't raise your voice.
- Use hurtful words.

CHAPTER TWO

Mind Tattoo

The way we lead our lives today, assimilate information, and think about things is in many instances through the eyes of yesterday. At birth we all start out equal with a clean canvas, with no previous exposure to the situations in front of us. As we begin to interact with our parents at home, peers at school, and co-workers in the workplace, however, we begin to develop a self-contained reality based on these experiences and interactions. All of this begins to accumulate and negatively impact us, and the things and people around us.

These experiences are etched into us as a "mind tattoo" that remains with us today. Mind tattoos form the perceptions we have about the world and ourselves. They are an unconscious part of us that dictates all of our thoughts and actions.

Let's say we have been diminished by one of our parents. This could be due to one parent leaving the other, words spoken over us, a parent's neglect because of work, or just our own general sense that a parent was not supportive or present emotionally. A child may interpret these scenarios to mean that he or she lacks value. This may sound minor, but to children who have experienced it, it can become a mountain in their hearts. Yet the way we feel is always a result of how we have chosen to feel because of another person's words or actions. When we interact with someone who doesn't give us the attention we expect or crave, this may also trigger a mind tattoo that puts us into a reactive mode. It's important to remember, however, that our reactions to another person's actions or comments are really us reacting to something within ourselves. It's an old wound that, when triggered, gets activated.

The two most likely outcomes when we go into a reactive mode are avoidance or anger. At that point, we are no longer in control of our present—our mind tattoo is in control. This means that instead of viewing an experience as it really is, we label it according to our past perception of an outcome of a previous experience.

A lot of us are unaware of why we feel bad. The bottom line is that whatever happened in the past we cannot change, just as when we set our vehicle's GPS on a journey from A to B, we cannot change the intangibles that may present themselves to us during the journey. We can only change the way we handle ourselves in situations. We can change the way we deal with problems, how we interpret them, feel about them, and ultimately move through them. In other words, we have a choice of whether we are open or closed to new possibilities.

Taking Things Personally

Someone may look at us, not in a demeaning way, but we perceive it as such. A person may not have time to meet with us, which doesn't mean they are insulting our importance. Or they may need to take a phone call while in our company, which could be seen as undervaluing us, even though they are just living out the everyday routine of their lives.

Although, we may not be aware of this fact, most of us hear a voice, if not several, going on in our heads most of the time. This is an involuntary dialogue, a one-man show that most of us spend our entire lives in without realizing that we can stop it. You may have experienced a person who has been wandering around and living in the streets for a number of years who appeared to be talking to himself. That's not too dissimilar to you or me, only we don't speak it out loud.

This is the voice of our enemy, the saboteur that resides in our deepest midst. It is the one that judges, compares, brings you down with negative self-talk, likes, and dislikes, etc. This is what I refer to as our Mind TiVo, a script that plays back experiences from our past into our present situation, or one to come. It perceives things mostly through negative stored information. This is because the human brain has around 60,000 thoughts per day with 90 percent of those thoughts repeated, and 85 percent of these being negative. It is by this process that you find yourself worrying or stressing as your mind continually plays a home movie of all the "what if" and "if not" scenarios. Even if you are thinking about things relevant to your current situation, it is most times through your interpretation from the past. This is due to your mind having been conditioned and molded through cultural and societal paradigms. So you see and judge the present through the eyes of the past, and get a totally distorted view of it. It is not uncommon for the inner voice to be a person's own worst enemy. Many people live with a nemesis in their head that continuously attacks and punishes them, draining them of positive energy. Not only does this predicate a life of stress and turmoil, but it also contributes to the meteoric rise in present-day diseases. The battle is never in the circumstance, but instead dwells in your mind.

The amazing thing about your and my mind, is that it can be

reprogrammed much like a TiVo to play a brand-new script. This will free you to lead the life you want and not the one restricted by your mind. Start becoming aware of moments when you go into your head and the voices you hear. This usually takes the form of a pattern with similar thoughts occurring again and again within certain circumstances. When you become aware of the voice, try hearing it from the outside looking in, without determining what it means, instead just listening to what it says. If you edit it, you will be interpreting it from an inner voice and masking what it's really saying to you. As your awareness increases, the pattern is broken as you are no longer controlled by its prompting. You have become aware of your presence and consciousness, and therefore are no longer at the mercy of your thought patterns. Through the increase of awareness and consciousness, you will be stepping into the real you and leaving behind the false you in the rearview mirror.

In our dealings with others, this would help us to define ourselves independently, in place of being at the mercy of their reactions, behaviors, or circumstances. Doing this would transform our usual pattern of taking offense or creating a negative reaction to any one of the innocent scenarios that can otherwise be perceived as offensive. This would leave us to be open and at peace. A conscious participant as a opposed to an involuntary reactionary to life.

By removing the personalization of things, we become able to reshape our mind tattoo and move forward with our lives in a smoother fashion. This makes all the difference between moving forward and walking in a circle. When we move forward, our life moves with a purpose, instead of leaving us stuck walking faster and faster in the same learned patterns of cyclical negativity. We are unburdened with self-imposed baggage and find ourselves lighter and freer to go on living.

Limiting Beliefs

There is a story of a bear that had lived in a zoo all his life and was transferred to a large animal reserve. When he came out of his cage, he would only walk 10 steps to the right and 10 steps to the left. Even though he now had abundance, his mind had limited him to a small space because of his past. Do you see how detrimental this type of thinking can be? Do you see how we sabotage our lives by leading them in this way?

Our life is constrained by our individual self-contained reality. Cynicism, negativity, and stress create limiting beliefs, learned behaviors, and thought patterns that we accept and live our lives by. But we can transform our thinking. Our thoughts and behaviors are mostly cyclical, as different situations arise and trigger the same cycle of negative thinking, behavior, and feelings. Most of us take that cycle with us wherever we go. We can be on a relaxing island vacation, or buy a new home in a new state, or even move out of the country, and the same pattern will still repeat itself. This then becomes a shadow that can cloud and blank out even the most beautiful of azure skies. Our vision and horizons become very peripheral.

Most of us seemingly go through a life seeing only a small amount of its greatness. The human mind can be at times much like a movie trailer with little flickers here and there of moments we have been conscious to in our presence and its fleetingness. With over 60,000 thoughts per day, it's hard to separate our thoughts from what is going on all around us. We can be thinking about our children who we have just dropped off at school, our next meeting or rushing to one, feeling stressed in heavy traffic, being content or discontent, focused, or blurred. All of that is like the contents of a mental TiVo. People record many things on their TiVos. Yet being present is not a TiVo, nor is it the things you leave stored on it. If we focus on slowing down our minds from 100 miles per hour, we can then begin to step into the comprehension that life is a series of passing moments that will be missed in all the mind's clutter. I can hear you saying to yourself "Sounds good, but how do I slow my mind down?"

Instead of being the victim of your ongoing thinking and mind-box clutter, you can also create a gap in the mind stream simply by directing the focus of your attention on what is immediately visible around you. Just become intensely aware of the present moment. This really sets you on a course of changing the way your mind functions and sees things. In this way you draw consciousness away from the mind's activity and create a gap of stillness, in which you are highly alert and aware, but not thinking. This slows the mind down from cluttered thoughts to clarity. In your everyday life, you can practice this by taking any routine activity that normally is only a means to expedite before going onto something else. It enhances more focused attention instead of an incessant blur. Otherwise, the mind is like a train going from one stop to another before exhaustion sets in by mid-afternoon. For example, every time you take a sip off coffee, put your focus on the shape of the cup and the color of its contents. Be totally present. Or when you hold your iPad or smartphone, be aware of its feel, texture, color,   the sound of sending a text messages, and so forth. Look at the outline of furniture and the texture of all the things around you. There is one certain way of knowing if you have slowed things down a bit ... How do you feel? More relaxed? More aware of things and the objects around you?

Similarly, we can divert an existing behavioral pattern and replace it with another one that serves us better.

Building awareness brings about the ability to recognize and divert unhealthy thought patterns to different, better thoughts. This can be as simple as reminding ourselves, "Maybe this was not against me." We basically need to get over ourselves and rise above to something higher. It is only when we change the way we see our circumstances, that we have the ability to change them through rising above them.

When we break away from this negative mind tattoo, we open ourselves up to the possibility of this being the greatest day. We see ourselves as being blessed with today, which is infinitely more significant than yesterday, because yesterday is gone and we cannot change our lives through yesterday. It is only from this present moment onward that we can affect our lives either negatively or positively. Many of us spend time thinking that the grass is greener for others, when the reality is that we create what we want the grass to be, because when we get to the other side, it will be just another version of today, unless we make the change from within. We can spend our entire lives arriving at a place or goal, only to find when we get there that it was all smoke and mirrors.

Regaining Power

A fundamental part of changing our reality is changing our core beliefs and values, as we cannot move forward with the same mind-set that got us to where we are today. If our thoughts remain what they have always been, then they will be just that, and we will continue to get more of the same in life. Once we replace negative thought patterns with positive ones, we'll start to see positive results.

When we experience feelings of anger, sadness, guilt, resentment, or regret, these thoughts are rooted in our projections and interpretations of the events that we have encountered. It is only by changing our focus to the awareness of the present moment that we can begin to regain our full power. This helps us bring about a feeling of calmness and peace, and by doing this often enough, we can become the new us: light and free. We can become more open to the possibilities today has for us and connect to the things that have, until now, been out of reach.

A lot of us get comfortable feeling bad because it is the only way we know how to feel. If a pig is in mud, even though the pig may not necessarily like the mud, he is too scared to try something new. The challenge is to find something else we may like more—something that may be the greatest thing we ever had. All we need to do is take the plunge and get out of the boat, as change requires doing something we have not done before. To get something different requires us first to be uncomfortable, but if the desire is greater to make a change, nothing can stand in a person's way.

Note: The mind is an amazingly powerful tool if you work it for your benefit. If not, it can prove to be your archnemesis and lead to a life of pain and struggle. The mind can control you, or you can control it—this is your choice. You believe that you are your mind. This is the veil. The mind has taken dominion over you.

Exercises

To help increase your state of awareness, start to slow down your breathing by counting from 1 to10, and transfer your mind onto your breathing rather than your mind chatter, as this will aid you in becoming more aware of the present moment. Focus on the objects around you: tables, chairs, bottles of water, coffee cups. If outdoors, notice the sky, trees, and the subtle sounds. Begin to notice the uniqueness of each object and the space it occupies, as this will give you a feeling of spaciousness and calm. The feeling that everything is one big blur will be diminished, and in its place you will gain an awareness of the present moment as something vivid. The stress-filled mind with its chaotic self-chatter will begin to diminish. You will notice that the tired, drained feeling you have at the beginning or end of each day will instead be one of enthusiasm and energy. This is because living with negative thoughts is draining and takes away from all that is joyful. The great thing is that we can make changes now. We have choices and opportunities to arrive at new ways of thinking and a new lifestyle. It is completely up to us what we want to do.

CHAPTER THREE

The Power of Thoughts

The thoughts we have are more powerful than we can understand or comprehend as they become the incubators for all our actions. They impact every cell of our bodies. What's even more significant is that the thoughts we have also impact our hearts. As we read in the Bible, our actions are ultimately a mirror of the condition of our hearts. So how we are in our hearts is how we are in our actions. That means if you want to change your way of living, you've got to first change your way of thinking.

Very often therapy and counseling deals with the symptoms and behaviors, but very clearly it's the heart that predicates all human behavior, good or bad. This encompasses all areas of our behavior from the way we think, react, and respond to people and situations in our daily lives. So the way we think about things is from our interpretation of how we, as individuals, see things. It is the synthesis of our spirit and our soul. Our actions are simply a mirror of what's already in our hearts. The condition of our hearts will directly be mirrored by what is going on in our business or personal lives. So, very simply, what's happening on the inside will manifest on the outside.

If we feel depressed, bitter, self-loathing, angry, or have a poverty mind-set, we need to course correct our hearts. Nobody can make us feel a certain way in life, as the way we feel comes from our own choice and free will. What controls our minds or the synthesis of our spirit and soul—is what controls our lives. Control is to exercise authoritative or dominating influence. It is to direct. Whatever is directing my mind, from the way I think or feel about something, is going to direct my life. This is why it is not the circumstance that we struggle with most; it's our mind-set in that circumstance. The mind is the battlefield, so the quality of life that we live is determined by the quality of mind that we have.

"In essence, our life is what our thoughts make it; therefore, if we can ever change our way of thinking, we can change our way of living." This sounds straightforward, but it is much more complicated and complex. I believe that one God moment with divine illumination and revelation can set us on a course to bringing a permanent change. If we want a quality life, and how many of us would say, "I want a quality life?" then we have to have a quality mind. (Cited inspiredpreaching.com)

The key element to change is in the awareness that the mind we have is our false mind. It is not the one God gave us, but the one our human state has imposed upon us. Our mind today is the product of everything we have experienced since being born. This has come through life experiences, parental influences, education, media, etc., which have conditioned us to think and act in our false (carnal) state. We are all created by God with a spirit mind, but as a result of our separation (carnality), we develop a mind that is controlled by the patterns of this world. It is therefore at the mercy of every influence and trend. As soon as we become aware of this, we can begin to renew our minds and then be reunited with God (our maker), being then influenced by the Spirit of God.

As we are all born into free will, we find ourselves engaged in a daily struggle, a battle between a carnal and spiritual mind. We find ourselves and our minds controlled by our five senses: what we hear, see, smell, taste, or touch. This process is known as sensory living. What is revealed is that our daily battle is between our separated (carnal) mind, which is controlled by our ego, and our spirit mind, which is in unity with God. How this works out in our lives is that the worldly mind is predominantly one of pride, anger, lust, greed, and ultimate destruction, because it maintains itself by the "I" in us. On the other hand, the spirit mind that is the one intended for us, is completely juxtaposed, as it is one of abundance, peace, love, and living in unity with all creation. This sets the scene for a life that is very much in keeping with current societal norms and paradigms. We are striving to get, as opposed to thriving to give.

"Ultimately, of course, every outer purpose is doomed to 'fail' sooner or later, simply because it is subject to the law of impermanence of all things. The sooner you realize that your outer purpose cannot give you lasting fulfillment, the better. When you have seen the limitations of your outer purpose, you give up your unrealistic expectation that it should make you happy, and you make it subservient to your inner purpose." (Cited yourpagemaker.com)

The key to understanding how this tug of war within our minds works is to have an awareness that we are in control of our minds. We are stewards in charge of what goes in and what goes out. We cannot put the blame on how we think or feel upon the shoulders of others. To make a lasting change, we need to not blame our childhoods, schooling, perceived lack, society, or the current times, and instead look at ourselves and begin to make the changes from within. God made us stewards because if it were not so, then somebody else would get to dictate the thoughts and actions of our lives, then they could control our destinies.

Circumstances can make us angry but cannot make us bitter. We can choose to let the anger go and use it to become a better person. We don't have to be full of anxiety, depression, fear, or take on a false mind of poverty or limitations. You are fearfully and wonderfully made, a God masterpiece with His divine plan and purpose both in and through you. You can have much more than you can think or imagine. You can change your way of living, if you first change your way of thinking.

Those are choices and decisions that I will daily struggle with, but I am going to show you how you can overcome and live the victorious life, through transforming your mind to be spirit-driven.

If I am responsible for the stewardship of my mind, Proverbs 4:23 says "Keep thy heart (the intertwining of your soul and your spirit, it is your mind); Keep thy heart with all diligence for out of it flow the issues of life." The word "keep" in Hebrew means to guard and to protect. We are to be gatekeepers to protect the opening of our minds.

Get an image? What does your life look like in five years? What does your life look like in 10 years? I want you to see yourself. Are you whole? Are you happy? Do you have restoration? Are you healthy? Are you fulfilling a purpose?

Are you moving in all that God ordained for you to be? Are you as a head or a tail? Are you put together fully for the purpose that God created you to be in the first place?

I want you to get a visual image. Can you see it right now? Here is what it says: "As a man thinks, so he is at last in his actions." So in 10 years, if I don't like the quality of my life, I don't get to blame everybody else. I have to look back.

What did I plant as a seed in my life earlier that brought into fruition what is in my life today? If we don't like it, as there are times that we didn't guard our minds and permitted what people said or did to hurt, limit, and restrict us, then we can overcome and take them out so that they don't have to remain a part of our lives. We need to take some things out of our minds before we can transform them.

We have to be gatekeepers to protect the opening of our minds: what goes in and what comes out. The Bible goes on to say "with all diligence," and this is crucial: "with all diligence as characterized by steady, earnest, and energetic effort." It means persevering application, so it is not something that is osmosis: So if I am to have a Spirit mind, I have to have persistent application.

In the same way that what you think today is as a result of habits that you have developed, the new way that you can think will also come through the creation of habits. In this case, a new habit. You need to change the things you do, in order to change the life t you have settled for. To change by hearing you need to change the things you listen to. This means not making the news media your main source of information. The world opinion and its media are based on a limited, negative, interpreted view. Focusing on this will not bring your mind into renewal, but will feed the false you through its negative, limited view. You will remain in a negative, restricted way of living. It will give you fear, which is faith, but faith in the wrong things. In order to change your life, you need to focus on God's Word, as it is like a human operation manual. When you buy a new car, the controls and their functions are different than the one you had before. You touch and push things that are in new and different places. Because you follow the manual, you get what you want. In the same way, to change ourselves, we need to look at and listen to a whole different record. Listening to positive things such as inspirational speakers on web archives and reading inspirational writing and blogs. Reading the Word of God will give you the ability to see and feel things in a different way, to give you the life that He intended for you. Why settle for your best? It's a false best that has been distorted through focusing on the things of a separated world. Why not get His best, and the one He intended for your life? To become a new person you need to put your eyes and ears on the things of the Spirit every day, much like what you have done until now on the news media and what people say! Remember, whatever you focus your eyes and ears on will become your life.

Romans 12:1 and 2 say in the King James, "Do not be conformed to this world, but be ye transformed by the renewing of your mind, so that you may prove what is the good, acceptable, and perfect will of the Lord."

In other words, live in a way that is different from the ways of this world. Not just your life on Sundays, but your daily business, commuting, socializing, and walking around in life. This means not becoming too adjusted to the angry, vengeful, impatient attitude that is prevalent in the world and its people. Don't be so influenced by the patterns and ways of culture that you just conform without thinking. This would make you the product of what's around you by the way that you think. Imagine this, if we walk into a room full of smoke with a new sweater then sit around a while before we leave, the sweater has taken on the environment and now smells of smoke. By thinking in a new way, you will be the influencer of all that is around you, instead of being influenced. You will be changed from the inside out.

Change can only come from the inside out, as we can only see things in a different way if we change our internal mechanism, or operating program. How you think or feel about something will be mirrored by the way you see it. So if I want to change whatever is manifesting in my life, I've got to first change the way I see it. I've got to change the way I'm thinking, to change what I am looking at.

How are you transformed? By the renewing of your mind.

Renewing means renovation. Renovation is a complete change for the better. It means the act of improving by renewing and restoring, the state of being restored to its former condition. This is by acts or actions. What this really means is that we need to work to make a change that will only result with consistent application. It's not going to occur from the flip of a switch or a resolution, but with a conviction to pursue change by using the hunger predicated from our present discontent. How new or fresh do you want your life to become? The greater the desire, the greater the potential is for change for the better.

Our minds and the way we think today have been formed by many years of worldly conditioning. This process began from the moment we were born, and continued with our parents, what people have said about us, our culture, the news media, our environment, our circumstances, and life experiences. Then what, in effect, happens is we throw it all into a mixer (our minds), it then gets blended and through time forms as a deep mold, which then shapes our lives through the way that we think, and ultimately the way we find ourselves living today.

This often has not brought us the best of life. The best of life is in our spirit minds. This is one of zest, joyousness, love, and endless opportunity, empowering you to live a life that is beyond horizons. We need to rid ourselves of our old ways in order for the new to have space to come in.

As we have gone on in our lives, we have all experienced disappointments from other people. It could be from words used against us, physical abuse, neglect, betrayal or broken promises. The effect of all these experiences gets stored in our cells, and with it brings some broken parts in us. It is from this brokenness that we bring brokenness into our marriages, workplaces, children, driving on the streets, and in the way that we deal with life in general. In order to make a lasting change, we need to refresh, restore, and make new. Medicating and doing things to numb the pain may make a temporal difference, but we need to change the mind for a lasting solution. It is out of restoration that the pain can be washed away and the mind made anew.

The process of renewal is to get back what was once there. Insofar as the human mind, it's the restoration to its former condition. This is before the abuse, the family dysfunction, the betrayal, and the falseness of culture and patterns.

To really get a hold of this process and expand your life beyond your current horizon, you need to bring about the awareness that you are a spirit being wrapped up in a human shell. A spirit being having a human moment before going into eternity. The mind you had when you were born was one of the spirit, but through living in this world became separated from spirit (God), and then became carnal. This is the state that by taking on a false you (carnal identity), you took on a life of struggles and limitations.

Within this state we go on to live a life of limitation as we have taken on what society has said, or labeled of us, and not what has been decreed or declared over us. We had a spirit mind and need to get it back in order to live our lives without limitation and fulfill all that was planned for us as our real identity. This process can only occur in the way a caterpillar becomes a butterfly, by peeling the temporary cover away. How many of you want to peel this away?

To get your original mind back, you need to go back before your human mind TiVo, (stored information that has now become your enemy), which is your world mind that has predicated your false you. You've got to get back the real you, how you really are predestined to be. This is before you experienced disappointments, betrayal, harsh words, news media, or anything that is not from God. Remember, the way you think in the present has become your life. So, to change it, you must first change the way you think.

To begin the renovation, you need to start by becoming aware of all your negative thoughts and habits that are not serving you. They are all distortions and must be exposed in order to be conquered. In order to make a complete change and get your real mind back, it needs to be aligned to that of the one God gave you.

Thoughts are habitual. We need to be habitual to create new thought patterns. We are then able to adjust our lives. Thoughts encompass our entire lives, as we have upward of

60,000 per day, of which 90 percent are repeated the next day, with 85 percent of those being negative. You see how important it is to be aware of habits and patterns. All of life is driven by our thoughts. So if you want a better life, you need to create better thoughts. What we think becomes what we say, and what we say becomes how we live and act.

The challenge in this is not in the change, but the backdrop of our busy lives that we lead. The present-day lifestyle is full of distractions. Our electronic devices, although a blessing, can also breed the enemy of distraction. We give permission to have our minds bombarded with views and opinions, which are mostly worldly interpretations sowing seeds of limitations into our lives. With all of the noise and distractions, we need to make a very deliberate action and choice to cut it out. You need to first take out the noise, so you can hear God's voice. You will then be able to see and hear more clearly. Without the backdrop of all the noise, you will be able to connect to your real mind and who you were meant to be. The noise that brings with it false interpretations, labels, and bondage to a limited mind-set will be overcome and put to death. Do you want to live as a victim or a victor in your story? You are not a product of society, but a product of what God made you to be.

When you cut the noise out, you can be reminded of who you really are. You are not what cultural opinion, with its "norms" and sheep mentality, has influenced you to think. It's within an attitude of alignment that the false you will no longer have dominion on your life. When you start to live in alignment with the Creator, you start to think and act the way that was predestined for your story. The real you is revealed, and you begin to think and live a whole new way. Within this process, your thoughts bring impossible to be possible, pain to healing, sorrow to joy, and limitation to a thing of the past. You begin to live, not within the restrictions that you have been conditioned to, but the specific plan and purpose for your life.

What you hear loudest is how you will decide to live your life, as this takes dominion over your thoughts and actions. The meaning of dominion of your mind is that nothing controls you, as this is the predominant control. If you were created in the likeness of God, it means that you can think and act like Him. This is so powerful that it is life- changing. If you are ready to take dominion over your thoughts, your life can be transformed from the inside out. So if you change your mind, you can also change your actions.

By refocusing your mind on what God has said about you, and not society, you embark on a course that will take you to a whole new level. Being in His likeness means thinking and acting like Him. When you read and listen to different material, The Word, and inspirational music, you will be renewing and feeding the mind with higher-octane fuel. If you have a racecar, would you use the lowest quality fuel or the best to win a race? You would use the best. In order to have a better life, in the same way as the racecar, you would be required to put in the best. You can then pull every stronghold down (the thoughts that have restricted you). You can then realign yourself with God's plan and purpose for your life. This will be the reclaiming of your divine destiny. A right mind will be the right life. If God made you, isn't it better to think and function the way that He designed you to? If I buy a new car, I first read the operating manual to be able to get the most out of my new car.

With thoughts that renew your mind, you will no longer be at the mercy of changing circumstances or the ebbs and flows of life. Having your identity will mean that there is now a constant, or sameness, about you. You'll be independent of the world and its changing views, economically, socially, or culturally, as when it is based on all these variables there is a neurosis that comes with all this uncertainty. That's why sleep medication and antidepressant use is on the rise. Over the past two decades, the use of antidepressants has skyrocketed. One in 10 Americans now take an antidepressant medication; among women in their 40s and 50s, the figure is one in four. (The New York Times report, August 2013)

In aligning yourself with God's character and central nature, there will be no identity crisis, because you will have found your genuine you. It will be hard to have unforgiving thoughts, as God's character is love. You will have less anxiety, as you will not be depending on people and their changing moods and desires. Your peace will be as a result of depending on the invariable, in a variable world. You will be dependent and reliant on a God who is the same yesterday, today, and forevermore. As I am sure you would agree, the world is dysfunctional. In our relationships, morally, economically and culturally, there is a pear-shaped nature and quality to it all. Why not try getting back the purpose you were created for? Give it a try for a year, as I am convinced that you will have a more rewarding journey, with greater joyousness and more peace than you can explain or comprehend. Relationally, in your private or business life, you will be transformed from the inside out.

The product of believing our false inner voice is that we start to take on the false thoughts we have as being real. We become molded after years and years of living this way. We experience bouts of depression. We experience anxiety. We feel that we are less than we were created to be. We then get hopeless and discouraged. Does this sound like you at times? This is the false you preventing the real you from shining brightly.

The real issue is that we have believed the lies over the truth. Our inner voice, through all the years of making so much noise and clatter, has become our false reality. We have been so preoccupied with our mind chatter that we have not been able to see or hear clearly. We have become a product that our mind has edited from what we've heard.

If you have been born in the likeness and image of God, then the false you is your enemy. It's not your circumstances. Your race. Your height. Your age. Your finances. Your background. Your divorce. Your past. It's your mind and what you have taken on as being the truth. What you believe your life to be is all a deception and has taken you away from your best you. The real you is far greater than the one you are resigned to live.

The issue is that it is easier to live as a victim than a victor. We feel it's easier to fit in with society and how our experiences have shaped us. We therefore stay in the box. We feel it's easier to blame others for our challenges, our mistakes, and our shortcomings. This puts us in a mold. It may be easier to blame others, but to live the rest of our lives that way becomes, in reality, much harder.

What prevents more people from finding their real self is that it takes perseverance, diligence, and the fearlessness of being different. Conforming to the patterns of this world and ticking yourself on a list as "normal" takes no effort. Remember, our human nature gravitates to what is easy, not better. This is why most of us enroll in a life of mediocrity. It's plain easier. But is it ultimately what you want? Don't you want better?

We are stewards of our own lives. We are responsible for what we become. If we are not content with our lives today, we need to make changes for our life to be different tomorrow. We need to see things differently in the present, for them to be different in the future. The present vision needs to be forceful enough to mold your present.

So my self-concept, the way that I see my world, represents the core view I have of myself in the world. You cannot change how you see yourself in this world until you change your thinking. You can only change your thinking by what you put your eyes and ears on. This is what you identify in and hold as your reality.

How did you get to the place you are now? By identifying and focusing on certain things. You then took them onboard as being your identity, your self, and your reality. Why do you keep feeling bad, unaccomplished, or dissatisfied? Depressed? Regretful from past decisions or mistakes? Wonder how this can change? If you start to look at things in a different way, you'll start to see them differently. If you focus on positive things and reinforce how you were created in God's image and character, you will have the possibility of the best life. Our best is not the best, as it's one of our own editing. God's best is, as it's the one He created for our unique plan and purpose for our lives.

The things we have experienced throughout our lives, from the acts or words that have been spoken over us, have become mirrors of how we ultimately view ourselves. Our view is not always clear. as our emotions are involved. This is often inaccurate and then forms an inaccurate mold of us. Are you starting to see how this can set us in the wrong direction in our lives?

By using other people as mirrors, be it parents, teachers, siblings, new media, etc., they have given us a false mirror of who we really are. We believed a mirror that we took on to be our likeness, but not who we really are. This mirror is very deceptive in the way it maintains itself, as we take the things that feed us from it. Let me explain.

As the mirror reflecting into us, we saw an image that is not necessarily a true picture. This is where it gets interesting. When the reflection was negative, the imprint leaves a false you. When it was positive, be it from a parent or teacher, it made you feel accepted, valued, or worthwhile in some way. This then maintains itself as a snowball going down the mountain. As your life continues, the falsities of your beliefs about yourself continue to surface. This is how the thoughts many of us suffer from are born into existence. Even though not true, the "I am not worthy of this," " I'll never amount to much," "I am stupid," "I am ugly," "If I can't beat them, join them," "I am lonely," "I am ashamed" thoughts are created in our minds. I could take the rest of this book to write down all the false you thoughts, but I am certain that you get the point by now.

It's not a matter of deserving because there is nothing that all the money in the world could buy to put around you that is worthy enough of the value of who you really are. Life will lie to you, and people will make you feel like you are not accepted, like you shouldn't live in that neighborhood, you shouldn't go to that school, you shouldn't be a doctor or policeman. To understand this more, the real enemy is not our experiences or the people. The enemy is always our minds. The inner self is the battlefield to a greater life. What we think is ultimately what we attract from the outside. We need to change what we think from the inside, to change how we feel about the outside. You are fearfully and wonderfully made, a masterpiece. You are unique. You are one of a kind. When we begin to think like this, we begin to feel like this. Get it?!

When we bring down the molds that have kept us in a stronghold, we find that the resistance we had to change becomes diminished. This is what I find when speaking about God, that people immediately label me as "religious." "Godology" is about love and purpose. Religion is often doctrine. In our strongholds, we close all things down as "religion." That keeps us stuck trying to over study, overwork, over sex, over drink, over travel, etc. I think you get where I am going. We are in an unconscious state of desperation in trying to find, love, self-worth, or meaning.

God is not about religion; He is about relationships. The world and its obsession of labeling everything is a hierarchy. First class. Economy class. This level, that level, are all things that if you permit them, will keep you down. When you connect to your intended plan and purpose for you, it is just that: for you. There will be no more competition. It will be a life of contentment, as you will be at one with your purpose. The one intended for your life. Religion keeps you on the outside, relational keeps you aligned (inside).

I can't change something unless I know how it began. A mold is a mind-set that is resistant to change, a fixed thought process. In order to change my thought process, I must see how it is formed.

There are three ways that it is formed: 1) Perception. This is your understanding of what you have seen. 2) Perspective. A mental view or outlook. 3)Paradigm. This is a measure, perspective, or set of ideas. A paradigm is a conditioned attitude in the way you think of something based on your past experiences. Most people are unable to think outside of their paradigms or frameworks.

You've got to recognize that not all faults are truth. Our faults are not always truth because some of the framework has been formed in a faulty way. Some of the ways I see things, the reason I see things, are often through other people's opinions. It is not always accurate.

Yet many of us continue in a life that brings us sadness. We have taken onboard what was acted out or said over us and then made it our reality. This has become our false self. It is only within an awareness of this that we can begin to make any changes. It is like the blind leading the blind if we don't first gain an awareness. When reason is revealed, the solution will also be revealed.

We can choose to take ownership of our minds and connect to a positive way of thinking (Spirit), or remain controlled by the world and its patterns (carnal), negative, or limited. The former connects us to peace, love, and unlimited purpose (life), while the latter to cynicism, pain, anger, and regrets (death). Once you take ownership of your true mind, you are no longer a product of your past. You take on the you that you were created to be. You become your real self. You gain a spring in your step. You gain a joy in just being a part of a brand-new day. You start to not need sleep medication, as you are not drained after another day of frustration, regrets, fear, or anxiety. You don't need antidepressants, as you are no longer depressed about your circumstances. You are no longer a victim of your circumstances; you are a victor in your circumstances. You get stronger when challenges arise as you rise up and take life on with the original spirit and power God put in you.

You will then lead a life of divine alignment, and with it peace, abundance, joy, and purpose. With persevering application, this will become your new way of thinking, as you will be empowered to do all that your life is set to do. Within alignment, your crooked path will be made straight. This replaces struggle with achieving purpose. Any negative, old way of thinking needs to be defeated with the positive. The light always expels the dark.

If I have spoken to your heart, please try to get the real self back. You will be amazed by how great you really are!

CHAPTER FOUR

Habits

The choices we make today stem from the time we first started to make them. We don't do them just because we decided to do them today. We get into a habit of living a certain way. A habit is a behavior that becomes part of us through repetition. Very simply, if somebody has a habit of being untidy, that's something that they've developed. It's coming from how they feel within themselves, but it's also one of the habits they have created. For example, if a person hoards all kinds of things in their car, it is likely that if they kept a rental car for three or more weeks, that it would look exactly the same way as their own car. There is a reason for all behaviors. People who hoard may have a stronghold in an emotional area of their lives, want to avoid making decisions, or are perfectionists who want to avoid making the wrong decision. This is also a good indicator that they grew up within an unsettled, insecure home. This behavior is then their mirror of that unsettled state they feel from within that has now manifested from their childhood.

Your quality of life today is very much determined by how you have dealt with all that has passed before. How content you are comes from the habits of what you focus your eyes on. How sound or unsound you are is from your diet, what you put into your body—not only through your mouth, but also your eyes and ears. What you do on a daily basis forms the things you believe in, and from that, the person you choose to be. In effect, your habits become your life.

For example, let's focus on the habit of lateness. I think it is safe to assume that most of us, if candid, would say that being late is inconsiderate to those it affects, but this is not the explanation. There are several reasons for chronic lateness. The reason in most cases is a psychological one. This can be an unconscious reaction to something that was predicated from childhood. It can be to fill a void for attention. Maybe a sibling was seen as favorite. This came from the assumption of them getting more praise and attention. Maybe late persons enjoy the attention they get from making an arrival, then excitedly describing to the person or group of people waiting what a tough time they had getting there. This will usually result in a reaction of sympathy (at least from people who don't know that something or other always seems to detain them.) Or maybe they grew up with a parent or parental figure who was harsh and used their lateness to draw attention to themselves so they could feed their broken pieces with forgiveness and empathy. In some cases, it can also be that they are totally unaware or uninterested it what others think or feel when they are left waiting for 10, 20, or even 30 minutes.

It is good to assume that if we continue to do something on a regular basis, we are getting something out of it … we are! Let me break it down. Those who are chronically/habitually late, to a degree, have a perception that others do not think highly of them. This behavior is a passive- aggressive way of imposing themselves on a situation. This alludes to a sense of worthiness and control. It compensates for the lack or self-worth or control they are feeling within themselves, so that this behavior is then manifested on the outside. This can be on a conscious or an unconscious level.

Until we see our innate value (self-perception), we will not see the value that we bring to others (other-perception). This dynamic can go on and on until such time we make a change from within, as this is transactional social perception. Simply put, we are late to make us feel better. You could also ask "Why show up at all?" if you are habitually late for movies, meetings, or most other things, and that is indeed true. Showing up is all about being present, as being late all the time is part of a bigger picture, the inner fight of being present. Being present comes from an inner feeling of value. So that not being present reveals an inner voice crying out "I am of little value" to the meeting or whatever I am attending. You are working off a self-perception formed from the past, that we are of no value to the meeting we are going to in the future. So we have given dominion to the past to minimize and dictate our present. The false you is deceiving the real you.

How Do I Improve My Habits?

Develop an inner dialog with yourself, and begin to figure out which category best sounds most like you. Begin to move forward from that point. Look also at the bigger picture of your life in general. This could include your consistency with career, diet, and exercise. Your approach to lateness will not be the only area of your life that looks a bit skewed once you start to become aware of your patterns and how they are affecting you.

The positive or negative habits we have either move us forward or impact us in a detrimental way. For example, if I wanted to create a habit of moving forward, I'd create a structure to my life that would be complementary to the direction I would want my life to go in.

If I wanted to move forward in a business field, whatever

field this would be, I would create a habit of writing down all the goals I have in that area, as without goals, there is no meaning to our actions.

All the habits that you practice have one thing in common: they're repeated behaviors. They are things you have done on a regular basis. You have learned to incorporate them into your lifestyle. It is estimated that out of every 11,000 signals we receive from our brain senses, the brain consciously processes about 40 (Cited Medical Journal). So, a habit is really a lifestyle, whether it's excessive eating, smoking, going for a run, or brushing your teeth in the morning. It is a learned behavior. Habits are all part of a cycle, your brain going into automatic mode, and then the routine of doing the particular behavior itself. The part of the brain that is prominent in habit-making behaviors is known as the basal ganglia, located within the prefrontal cortex, affecting our decision-making process. However, when we are acting out of habit, our brains are on auto mode, with the conscious mind not in use. When a behavior becomes a habit, it triggers the brain to feel a reward, and this therefore sustains that behavior as a habit (limbic mind). Simply put, this means when we associate a particular behavior with making us feel good, we repeat it. The behavior then sustains itself for that purpose, even if destructive to us. That is how habits and addictions are formed. The other benefit of our brain going into auto mode is that it can almost completely shut down, which gives us the capacity to multitask and accomplish even more.

Habits form our structure as people and the way we conduct our lives, which shapes and molds our character.

The way we live our day today is the way we live our week, and the way we live our week is the way we live our lives. To break negative habits they must first be recognized as being detrimental to us. An awareness needs to be developed together with a conviction to make a change. Most people get stuck in the habit. "All of life is a habit until you die," as the saying goes. We must not get stuck in the habit, but instead see freedom in the change.

The goal is to be breaking habits that are not beneficial and replacing them with better habits. If we want to change a habit, we need to take action steps that will lead to that change. It starts with small, frequent action steps. Although small, collectively, they shape our characters and the way we live out our lives.

In order to change habits you no longer want, make a note of how you behave in certain situations. Start this process by noting, from the time you arise, the choices and activities you do on a daily basis. Your eating, sleeping, drinking, and working everyday life. Do you structure your day? Write and document your tasks within it? Include short-, medium-, and long-term goals?

After taking an inventory of your habits, write down the ones you want to change. To start this process, look at one habit at a time. For example, if it's timekeeping, finding yourself rushing to get to meetings you are mostly late for, you can make a simple change that will help you improve. If this occurs in the mornings, then you can set the alarm 15 minutes earlier, or during the day, set your alarm on your cell phone 15 minutes before you would usually leave.

Another habit many of us get into is starting to do tasks and only getting them half done. This can be painting a room in our house, laundry, yard work, writing Christmas cards, etc. This stems, not from having too many things to do or accomplish, but rather from not putting them in order of priority. There are only 24 hours per day, 168 hours per week, and that will not change. To be more effective, it's best to write a "to do" list in order of priority. This will prevent mind-clutter, while at the same time help you to be more effective with tasks that require your attention.

Set a goal of repeating any new behavior for at least 30 days, as I have experienced tremendous changes using this method. This has helped to create lasting habits in my life. To make yourself accountable, you can ask a close friend to help keep you in check. You will be amazed how this simple step can become a significant factor in spurring change. You can apply this principle to each habit you want to change, 30 days at a time.

In order to understand the way habits ultimately work, you must understand their framework and what sustains their existence. All habits start with a trigger, as this is what initiates the behavior or action, then the doing of the behavior or action itself. Lastly, the reward from doing the behavior or action is what sustains the behavior or action. This is known as the "Habit Loop," a three-step process to how all habits are formed.

There needs to be this framework for all the habits we do on a daily basis. The reason for doing the action, the act of doing it, and then the reward that sustains it.

Let's take a look:

—You get a text message from a friend asking you to meet for a run.

This initiates the behavior or action.

—You go to meet your friend at a specific time.

This actuates the behavior of running.

—The reward is that your fitness level improves. You then make your favorite treat meal a reward for keeping to your fitness schedule, affirming that you are well pleased with your result.

This basic structure repeats itself as the reward and maintains the habit of the doing of an action or behavior.

The challenge is that the same structure also applies in the formation of destructive behaviors and addictions.

So let's take a look at how you can structure new habits.

Don't depend on drastic resolutions, as these are fleeting and do not bring permanent change. The optimum way is to create a new habit around an activity that is already present in your life.

For example, I used to skip out on breakfast and just have coffee in the morning. So before going to bed each evening, I started leaving a bowl with some pre-measured oatmeal in it. I placed the bowl in front of my coffeemaker. This made it easy, as I didn't need to rely on motivation or memory. Having coffee was an existing activity, and this change acted as a cue to make my new behavior of including breakfast a habit. The result is that I have now created a new healthful habit of having breakfast. Adding an action step to the ones you are already doing makes it much easier to develop new habits. All new habits have one thing in common, they have to be started.

Choose the things you practice most on a daily basis, and then build around them.

For example, Trigger: Alarm wakes you at 6:30 a.m. Action: Get up and read affirmative blogs, scriptures, or listen to spiritual music for 15 minutes. Reward: Feeling uplifted.

Be empowered to be a victor in your challenges and not a victim.

For example, Trigger: Gas low light comes on. Action: Go to the gas station. At the same time, check oil/coolant and tire pressures. Reward: Better maintenance and lower repair costs.

These are just two very simple habits, as change is made first in the simple—the ones you can't say "no" to.

There may be need for some experimentation with various triggers to find which fits the change in behavior or habit you want to create. It may take a while before you can reveal a habit that is so automatic you cannot say "no" to doing it. You might have to ponder a bit before figuring out how to make your new habit so easy that you can't say no. The principle of positive affirmation as you go along will again take time to become a habit, as by nature we are generally very hard on ourselves.

I will not cover addictions in this chapter, but instead reveal them further in this work as you read.

Work out the habits in life that you really want to change, and before you know it, you will be living a whole new life. Don't focus on the sprint, as all of life is a marathon. We gather wisdom out of challenge, knowledge by our mistakes, to then do things more effectively. Out of loss, the greater appreciation we get of all we have. By seeing more of what is already great, you can begin to celebrate each day as the gift. The best day for us to start changing a habit that is not serving us is today.

Moving Forward

The concept of moving forward is about not getting stuck or derailed by sudden changes in our circumstances, which can affect our health, finances, employment, or loved ones. Any potentially life-changing event can happen within a moment's notice, and unless we build the right mental foundation, we can fall apart at the seams.

Life is cyclical, with time moving forward, while at the same time, not really allowing us to move forward with our lives. We go from one year to another expecting something to change, yet we still do the same things, think the same way, and walk around with the same learned behaviors that make up our unique perpetual circle. As the days turn into years, the only thing that changes is the calendar. We can only make a change if we become the change we are seeking.

Most of us essentially live our lives in a circle by making the same choices that trap us within the limitations we've imposed upon ourselves. Our potential is all too often what we have determined it to be through what we have experienced and the outcomes of what those experiences have brought us. We put this into our mind-box that more often shrinks our life into far less than it can be.

Until we become more aware, we navigate our lives through this self-contained reality. Ideally, we move forward with what was intended for us—moving through circumstances and using them to grow our understanding of what our purpose is. But the reality is that most of us get stuck by our challenges without ever making any tangible progress.

If we go through a tough time, which will often come upon us suddenly, we have to learn to withstand the storm. For example, if someone close to us passes away unexpectedly, or if we encounter a financial challenge, or a natural disaster causes damage to our home, we may feel helpless and at the mercy of our circumstances. Be aware that while we may not be able to change circumstances, we can work with them in a way that will allow us to overcome them and grow from them in a positive way. Ultimately, the way we view setbacks will determine how we move through them. All that we have been through has been in preparation for this very moment we are in now.

Ideally, we'll absorb the pain and move forward with the knowledge that whatever challenges we face have been put in our path for us to grow and learn from. The strength we have can only be measured by the challenges and circumstances that we have overcome. When we overcome a challenge and begin to heal, we gain greater resolve and determination, which are qualities that can be used to greatly improve our lives.

But before that, we need to accept the circumstances in front of us and then work on moving through them gracefully. We can do this by focusing not on the difficulty factor, but on the solution factor. When we fixate on solutions instead of problems, things begin to work out in our favor. For example, if we lose a job in a layoff, instead of dwelling on the variables that caused the job loss, make a list of all the things that can be done to find another job. This list can include writing a great résumé, going to seminars that are relevant to your industry, contacting headhunters, making personal connections, calling personnel directors, and scouting classified boards. Putting the focus on what can be obtained rather than what has been lost can be life-changing, as this method can be applied to most other circumstances as well. Remember that it is better to walk in a slow, straight line than faster and faster in a circle. A different outcome requires a different action.

In order to make a change, we first have to recognize what we're doing and then sit down and make a plan for how we will change it. Every change has to be predicated on developing an awareness of our present actions, followed by creating a detailed series of steps that will change those actions so that we may move toward an outcome we want. This will release our state of mind from bondage to freedom. Every day is a brand new day, a brand new start to life, as we can all make changes without waiting another minute.

Every moment presents an opportunity to make a change right now at this very minute.

Part of moving forward is asking ourselves: What am I doing each year? What is my purpose? What am I achieving? These questions have to be answered with a conscious effort. No change can be made without consciousness or honesty. The subconscious stores information from the conscious, so conscious change comes first. With enough time and practice conscious changes become part of us through our subconscious, which is what then determines our daily behavior.

As humans, we operate on two main mind-sets: fixed and growth. Both are thought patterns that we develop over years, though each leads to a very different outcome.

The fixed mind-set is the one most of us fall into. It's one that is primarily as a result of the false truths we have subscribed to about ourselves, others and life in general. It could be that we don't feel good about ourselves or our ability at performing a certain skill, telling ourselves we're not tall enough, are bad at relationships, are too fat, or even too thin. This is an adopted mind-set that cannot readily be changed, as it is not flexible.

While it's true that we all have unique gifts and talents to offer the world, the fixed mind-set is steadfast in its determination as to what is good or bad. It dictates a tendency for us to avoid doing certain things, which can add up to a whole host of missed opportunities over time.

The growth mind-set, conversely, is one that is open to learning and new opportunities and therefore sets us up to be receptive to everything the world has to offer. This translates into looking at challenges as new opportunities to advance and gain a deeper understanding of our purpose, which may fuel us to even greater heights. For example, if I am a divorcée walking around with a growth mind-set, I could see my divorce as a relationship that was no longer able to continue, but defines just a chapter in my life, not my whole life. If reinforced repeatedly, this outlook would become ingrained in my thought patterns as much as a fixed mind-set would. The deep-rooted limitations of the fixed mind-set can determine the outcome of an opportunity before that opportunity is given a chance to prove itself as being right or wrong. Overcoming it takes a lot of work.

When a fixed mind-set is turned into a growth one, we no longer fixate on an obstacle, but instead look at the solution. For example, if I believe I cannot be an outstanding public speaker, with a growth mind-set, I could translate that into a belief that I will become better by practicing. If we allow ourselves to become aware of the concept that there is a first time for everything and that people who are good at things are only that way because they started doing them repeatedly, our world can expand. We can open ourselves up to being more brave and daring, and very soon can be amazed by what we can do, particularly the things that our fixed mind-set told us we couldn't. The route to mastery can only be reached through doing. Fear breaks us down, while faith builds us up.

The fixed mind-set is usually a product of childhood, especially in regard to the things we've been told we did or didn't do well. Early criticism and praise set us up for life. If we were told as a child that we were clever at something, this can also set up a narrow belief system about the things we believe we are good at, causing us to focus only on those at the expense of a wide variety of other things that could have expanded our minds and hence our realm of possibilities. This may sound like a subtle difference, but the big comes from the small, and since we cannot see the small, we cannot see the big either.

Criticism and negative feedback can cause us to have a reduced belief in ourselves. The good news is that we can break the bad habits and thought patterns that have become our way of life. Start by opening yourself up by saying, "I can become good at doing whatever I set my mind to." Set up an action plan in priority of things you want to change. For example, if you find yourself being negative toward new opportunities, write down a positive-thinking action plan with the following affirmations: 1) I will be a positive person; 2) I will do all I can to be open to new opportunities; 3) I will always be ready to take on the challenge of something new.

The steps you can take to achieve this could include: 1) Try something new and different; 2) Document your results and achievements; 3) Set up a personal fine system in which you put a predetermined amount into a jar each time you are negative; 4) Hold yourself accountable to a close friend by letting him or her know of your action plan.

It also helps to put up a vision board in your office or home reinforcing all the things you want to do with positive affirmations. This will help rework a mind-set from "I am not good at this" to one of endless possibilities.

Become aware of situations when an inner voice says you cannot because you are "not good enough" and replace it with your new voice of "I can because I am good enough, so I will." Empower yourself by knowing that we all have a choice in how we interpret an opportunity. Negative thinking is also a choice, one that will keep us stuck. Only positivity will keep us moving forward. By building ourselves up by doing the things we have avoided, we can build an arsenal of confidence that very soon makes the once impossible very possible and real. Positivity can be grown and exercised like a muscle, in that the more we exercise it, the more it can act as a catalyst for change, growth, and a more enjoyable, rewarding, and fruitful life.

We should see ourselves like a bow and arrow, as our challenges force us to pull ourselves back to gather the power to let ourselves loose to pursue our divine destiny. If we can change our perspective about the challenges we face, we will see digression as progression. The things that we, as humans, feel are working against us are actually working for us, even if we don't see this at the time of the challenge.

CHAPTER FIVE

Why We Think the Way We Do

Ever wondered why we think the way that we do? We all start life with no prior experience and with nothing painted on the canvas. We then become influenced by the things around us: our families, society, the media, all creating an imprint on our minds. These imprints then form an automatic response to various circumstances, or events in our lives. The things we do on a daily basis are a part of our unconscious, habitual way of living.

The front of the brain, known as the prefrontal cortex, is

the rational and analytical part of our minds responsible for all the things that we think on a conscious level. However, the way we live on a daily basis is more like a car on cruise control, or a plane on autopilot. We are actually living very much on habitual thought patterns, influenced by the limbic or emotional mind. That filters through mostly negative things, as we are in a world that has a propensity to be negative. Very few of us indeed are dwelling on the positive experiences we have had. There are many positive experiences, but society is programmed to conform to the negative patterns of this world.

The way we are structured chemically, genetically, and then influenced by the news media are all things that condition us to be negative. Bombs, terrorism, divorce, rapes, all of the stuff that goes on in the world. Existentially it goes on, but when it forms our limbic thought patterns, it affects our opportunities. It can have a negative influence on a broad area of our lives our relationships, interactions with other people, the way that we live, and ultimately our quality of life. If we are living our lives through a haze of negativity, it is like a Picasso painting with a curtain obscuring the glory and the presence of what is there.

Our mind-box, which is our self-made reality, becomes our everyday thoughts and responses to all that is around us. We need to renew the mind and reprogram the limbic system, as this will change the way we respond to opportunity, relationships, circumstances, and indeed every area that can motivate us to live more rewarding and fruitful lives.

In other words, if we refocus with the conscious, we will be doing unconscious things in a positive way. The very first time we became negative, we just did it, we continued doing it, and it became the way we are now living. However, we can actually reprogram the whole mind much the same way by refocusing it. The way we are right now impacts our lives, as we are not really living because we are in the confines of this bondage that has created our present mind-set. Very simply, when you are in that mind-set, you are restricted and controlled and get much less out of the life that God created and preordained for you.

All of this can be reprogrammed using techniques that I will go into in this book. We only have one life and the way that we lead it is through the thoughts we have created, as those thoughts are part of our free will. In order to live the life that you have always wanted, you need to change your way of thinking. A new way of thinking will be a new way of living.

As human beings, we are composed of mind, spirit, and soul. It is the concert of the mind and spirit that dictates our life. The mind is what controls and directs our lives. The battles in life are not the circumstances we experience, but are in the mind. So the mind controls the quality of our lives. In other words, the habitual (limbic) mind is in control of our day-to-day thinking. Now we are really going to look at the way this all started. As I pointed out earlier, the limbic mind is like an airplane on autopilot as it does all the functions we want it to do without us making a conscious effort. When the pilot is in cockpit, he can choose to fly the plane at a certain speed and direction by putting it on autopilot. In this mode, it is just moving forward without any conscious choice of speed or direction on his part. It has already been programmed, so it just moves along with the information that has already been input. We are all born equal with no previous recollection of experiences. As we grow up, we become exposed to our parents, siblings, societal norms and patterns, and media, which all had their part in influencing us.

What we heard and saw became our reality. If I am told that driving a motorboat is dangerous, that can be taken as a reality. Therefore, in my mind-set, when I see a motorboat, without even consciously thinking, immediately there is a thought of danger. The limbic mind is an emotional way of reacting to something in the present that is usually from the past. It is not seeing something the way it is. Of course, a motorboat can be dangerous, but this should not immediately come to mind. The thing itself cannot be dangerous. A car is not dangerous. A plane is not dangerous. Drinking wine is not dangerous, but it is what we associate with our thoughts that can perceive something as actually being dangerous.

To give you another example, we had a spell of really warm

weather without a lot of rain. When you comment to people, "Oh the weather is great," and they reply with, "we need rain," his is the limbic mind, which is programmed to react to something in the present. Of course rain comes. It has been coming for 6,000 years. It is not unusual. When we slip into that mind-set, it really takes control of our minds on cruise control. That is really what runs our minds. The cruise control, limbic episodes happen in all things in life. It could be leaving the office with thoughts of, "Well, someone is going to put a lot of work on my desk, and I am going to be rushed and not able to do it." Like anything else, it is something we need to be aware of doing in order to make the changes happen in our lives.

Most of us are not aware of why we are thinking the way we are, as we have done it for so long that it has become our habitual way of thinking. It obviously puts tremendous restrictions on our lives. Even though we are moving forward with it, it is like the plan is moving forward on a predetermined course. This leads to an encumbered life of obstacles. The way to connect to a bigger life is to connect with the universe. To have confidence and faith in God that all things will be supplied, and whatever is in our lives now, will work for our future. If we view something for what it is, the page of a certain book for what it is, we stay in the present. We do not go into any panic mode, which is channeled through the past.

Things become much clearer, and we have a lot more clarity

in decision-making. To change this way of thinking, you have to go into awareness, or proceed to make a deliberate mind-set change. We have to gain the awareness of what we are doing now, and if it is not working, replace it with different thoughts.

Through creating a oneness with all that is in this very moment, we create the ability of being able to stay present and not obscured in the past or the future. The reason some of us stay in the past or the future is that all of the pain is in present. So we stay in the past, or we stay in the future. It is a learned way of dealing with things as a coping mechanism.

So when we deliberately change our minds, the conscious mind will eventually become the subconscious, which is the limbic. When we develop a higher consciousness, we will change the way we think about things and the way we do things. The payoff for this is that our autopilot will be our new way of thinking.

The automatic way of thinking will be positive and not negative. This is why there are positive and negative people. They are working through looking at things positively, and that has become their limbic way of operating, their autopilot way of operating. Negative people, who are the majority, unfortunately, are looking through what has happened before and how that may affect their futures.

Many of our emotional and health problems were started

by our way of thinking. It is widely documented in health reports that stress is one of the main causes of disease and premature death. Stress is not always a reflection of our external circumstances, but a mirror of our thoughts and internal learned mechanism. It's our individual internal mechanism that can turn small, everyday challenges into mountains. This then triggers anger, frustration, anxiety, and depression. So it's in how we self-edit and mind-box our daily circumstances that determines the quality of our path.

As our mind has many layers, so our thoughts encompass many layers both in the conscious and subconscious realms. It is our subconscious that can cause so much pain and angst in our lives. This is due to our subconscious being part of a pattern that has developed over a long period of time. There are clear or subconscious thoughts. For example, a person is going on a roller coaster and dislikes heights, he or she may be fearful of getting hurt. On a more subconscious level, a person may be going on a date and think that the other person may not find him or her attractive. This is coming from a less clear place, and often from long-held ideas that stem from depression and low self-esteem. The most important part of dealing with negative thinking is raising your awareness.

In an anxious or depressed state, a person can only be negative even if all that is around them is positive. It is these strong feelings that effect the external situation, regardless of the circumstances or challenges that come. When these thoughts occur, they are automatic and arise without a conscious effort. We have about 60,000 thoughts per day, and 95 percent of those are repeated. Out of those thoughts, 80 percent are negative. These are referred to as (ANTs), or Automatic Negative Thoughts. A few negative thoughts may not impact a person too much, however, if we have more than a few, they can repeat and repeat and add up to be very detrimental indeed. It is just like having one ant in your kitchen instead of an entire sink full. The more ants, the more problems.

It's good to gain an awareness of when our negative thinking occurs. If we know when it is most likely to happen, we can start upon a course of minimizing the circumstances or environments that trigger this type of thinking. Negative thoughts act as a spiral effect, as once they filter into our thinking, they create a false reality of sadness, negativity, and despair. The more we have them, the more they become the snowball effect gathering strength and reality as we dwell in them. So it's important to minimize the negative pattern of thinking, as it will become a negative lifestyle and destroy the potential within you.

Like anything else, we have free will and can take on board anything as being true, good, or evil. Hoping that negative thoughts will go away will not work, as when a situation or circumstance arises that triggers them, they will rear their ugly heads once more. They cannot be sidestepped or avoided, as the nest of negative thoughts will always be festering and ready to take your mind over. It is only within an awareness that a strategy for minimizing can be started. It is more advantageous to work on breaking negative thought patterns at times when you are feeling your best, and not a times when you are in a downward spiral. Becoming conscious of our inner voice (enemy) and the cycle of what it tells us and when it occurs is very important. This gives you the ability to recognize the lies and circumstances that trigger them most.

Most negative thoughts are cyclical. They are the same negative, destructive words triggered by the same external conditions. They are an internal manifestation of an external false revelation. A false belief of something that has been manmade by our own mind. What makes it more of a challenge is we actually believe it to be true. So it's the way we think and feel about something that creates the reaction to it and not the situation.

For example, we may walk into a movie theater after the program has started and think that everyone is looking at us, with mind-chatter such as "I am disturbing people," "I am always doing stupid things," or "They think I am a nuisance." These are all reactions within ourselves as opposed to the situation making us feel a certain way. The situation cannot make you feel any way, but the way you feel about it can.

Another example is of arriving late to a party and feeling that this makes a person more important, or the center of attention. This is a perfect scenario of a false thought pattern. Others in the situation may have a completely different view. This is a reaction to society and our false perception and not the existential. The mind paints a thousand pictures, and we get sucked in by the enemy that seeks to kill and destroy. When you step into the realization that all of your negative thoughts are a fraud, you can begin to conquer this negative mentality.

Life and its unique Master Plan for each individual cannot be changed, but by changing your way of thinking, you can change your way of living. The type of thinking we do is a learned behavior. Depressed and negative people are not content feeling that way, but through the consistent adaptation of the mind, they are living with that mind-set. The challenge is that the more negative or depressed a person becomes, the more slippery the slope. It continues to spread like a cancer as the lies are held as truth. You need to lose your false self to find your true self.

Let's take a look at types of false negative thinking.

By becoming aware of the types of negative thinking, you can set yourself on a course to mind-correct your life.

Negative Mind Dominance

In this setup, the mind focuses on predominantly negative thoughts, ignoring or denying any positive ones that are present in reality. When a person focuses on the negative, they put attention to all their assumed failures and disappointments and what they perceive others think of them. For example, a person may recognize that a professor was not pleased with their application on a current exam but may ignore all the kind words of support that the same professor has shown them in the past. Another example would be a husband who feels he hasn't been a good husband by not giving his wife his attention recently. He has been stressed, overworked, and feeling below par. He completely fails to acknowledge the many times he has been there to nurture and support his wife.

To work on minimizing negative thoughts, write down occurrences when positive thoughts have been denied in turn for negative thoughts to show up. Do this for about four weeks, each time they show up, as this will help to gain an awareness so you can make changes.

Routine Pattern Thinking

In our human nature, we all get stuck in a routine within the course of our days and weeks. It is within this mind-set that we get accustomed to things being the way they are. Even during the times when one is achieving success and recognition, there is a tendency to ignore compliments and nullify any positive feedback. This can be due to getting adjusted to patterns, comparisons to other's achievements, or the inability to accept good. It is quite possible that a person can have academic, personal, and/or material success and still not accept or receive positive input from others or him or herself. These people have programmed their minds to nullify and deny all positive things due to having negative mind predominance.

Write down some examples of how you have nullified accomplishments, positive events, or compliments. If you do not recall a particular occasion, write down all the things that you have excelled in. Recognize how your mood changes as you recall positive or negative things. Are you more comfortable with negative or positive assertions?

The "Should Have, Would Have" Syndrome

Many of us look back at events in our lives with regrets and invite thoughts of "should have" or "would have." This creates a thought pattern in our subconscious that predicates anger, frustration, guilt, or depression. When directed and judged upon others, it can bring frustration and anger.

For example, if a person sees an elderly person coming out of a coffee shop and they don't think of holding the door open at that time, they may say to themselves after the fact, "I should have opened the door," "I am disappointed in myself." These feelings are likely to take on a hint of inadequacy or guilt. On the other hand, if a person cuts in front of us in a line at the grocery store, we may think to ourselves, "How selfish. They shouldn't have done that. They should have seen I was already in line." This is most likely to produce feelings of anger and frustration.

The word or thought "should" makes everything a self-judgment issue of right or wrong. It is a word that brings death to a situation. In effect, it is affirming that they, or the other person, is bad or in some way wrong. There are situations in life that are right or wrong. For example, a person burglarizing a home is most definitely wrong, and the word "shouldn't" is appropriate. However, for example, a tired husband may come home from a long day at work and may not notice his wife has been to the hair salon. When she points it out to him, he may say to himself, "I should have noticed." He may feel that he is bad or inadequate as a husband. While repeated lack of awareness of a partner will, in time, tarnish a relationship, as a one-time occurrence, it will by no means determine the true quality or character of a partner. However, taking on the affirmation "should" will make the person take on the false identity of being a bad or inadequate husband. This negative thinking pattern may cause tiredness and make the husband even less aware of things down the road. It is important to keep the "should" in our vocabulary to times when it is appropriate. We can either live our whole lives feeling that we are wrong, or chose to live the life that we were created to live. We need to let go of our false self, to then put on our true self.

Write down the "shoulds" or "shouldn'ts" that you have a habit of using against yourself or others. Take note of the circumstances that you are most likely to use them. Are they right or wrong issues?

Exaggerated and Dramatic Thinking

Life is a journey made up of many seasons. We must embrace that there will be smooth times and also times of great challenge. These can be emotional, financial, or physical. Some individuals are not well-equipped to embrace or accept the myriad of seasons. When things don't go the way they want, they tend to think their whole life is a disaster. This is when an individual loses sight of the fact that life is not all success or failure. There are good times and bad times.

When a person is caught up in this veil of lies, they build a small failure into a failed life, a small mistake into a total failure as a person, a disagreement with a husband or wife into the marriage is a total failure. This negative mind-set takes what is minor and builds it into a major catastrophe. There appears to be no intermediate balance between the two points, as it's triumph or disaster all the way. This permits for no flexibility with the ebbs and flows of life with ourselves, and also with our dealings with others. Life is not black or white, as it's about being flexible in the changing seasons, and learning that a challenge is a setup to greater things that are to come in your life.

When a person has this type of negative, depressed mind pattern, they are either on top of the mountain or all the way down. This predicates instability and deep periods of depressive thinking. There needs to be an acceptance of fluctuations, and the comfort to dwell in them. The joy and pleasure in life is in the ability to be fine and joyous in all the changes we can experience.

Write down occurrences when you have engaged in all-or-nothing thinking.

Mind-Box Limitations

This type of thinking restricts a person's future through a false limiting reality mind-set. This occurs when the mind paints a story of the outcome of any opportunity or life event before they have happened or been completed. It can very often be that a person hasn't even embarked upon them, and yet they have sabotaged the opportunity or life event that is in front of them.

This could be in the area of personal life, when a person starts dating someone new and paints a scenario for all the reasons the relationship would not work out. When completing work projects, a person may feel that their boss will think it's not good. Or when a person sets out on a long journey, they will think of all the worst-case scenarios, for example, missing a plane connection, bad weather, security problems at the airport, etc. As these are mostly predicated by a false mind-box, they are both restrictive and detrimental.

When a person has depressive tendencies, this creates a snowball effect by taking a significant role and influence in their everyday lives. They take on this false belief system, and actually become the life that they create in their mind. A person living with this self-made thought pattern is living a life of agony, restriction, and bondage to the enemy.

As we live the way that we think, and therefore become exactly what we think, writing a negative outcome in your mind of the opportunities coming into your life will often destroy them before they even manifest. The best way to combat this thinking pattern is to go through seasons of opportunity or changes and see what actually happens. By becoming aware of what happens, you will be able to see that many of your anxieties and negative thoughts about something were way off. The more you do this, the more open you will become to opportunities and the possibility of them being good. By taking the illusion off, you will find the truth.

Write down when you start to think of negative thoughts. This could be about things coming up in your personal or business life. It is important to log them, as you will then be able to compare what you thought would happen to what actually did happen. In time, this will develop as your personal arsenal to rescind any thoughts that create limitations or false beliefs.

Thinking Based on Feelings

This type of living is based on how you feel about things. It is out of permitting the mind-editing of events that have emotionally affected you and influenced you, to then take them on board as fact as to what your present reality is. Feelings are based on senses and emotions about how you think about something. When a person is governed by feelings, in a depressed state, their predominant thoughts and feelings are negative. This can stir up a whole box full of false beliefs, such as lack of self-worth, fear, or anxiety. In a depressed state, these feelings are magnified and made even more real to a person. It is paramount before a person can start to work on eradicating this unhealthful habit that they accept that it is just a falsely held belief based off an interpretation that has been made counterfactual by feelings.

Write down how you feel about things as they come up. This will give you a reference point to begin to identify how your feelings are impacting your life.

Taking Things Personally

This type of thinking involves the idea that everything relates to you. It is the perception that because of your lack or low value, that people are judging you negatively. In depression, which is when these thoughts most likely occur, there becomes a predominate thought that you are in some way drawn to seek the approval of others, compete against others, or feel that you are forced to do better than you can attain.

If a boss doesn't compliment a person for their work or says that he or she wanted something done differently, the person would then take it personally with the thought that they are not good enough, or in some way would need to seek the boss's approval. In a marriage, it could be that the husband buys a gift for his wife and then thinks that he is not good enough as he thinks that she didn't like it enough. Another example is when a person notices two people talking and they then look at them, they then think that it is something negative said about them. When a person assumes that any of these scenarios are about them, they have taken it personally.

This can originate from various places in a person's past, such as sibling rivalry predicated from a parent comparing your performance to that of a sibling. This is then mirrored within other human interactions in adulthood.

Write down examples of thoughts when you have taken things personally.

Building a Platform to Stop Negative Thinking

Example / Type of Thought

1. I am a complete failure.

—Exaggerated/Dramatized Thinking. "Complete failure" exaggerates a single situation. This is an all-or-nothing strategy.

—Negative mind dominance. Total failure overlooks any successes.

—Mind-box limitation. This thought puts a limitation, or mind-box, on your success.

2. Bad things are always going to happen.

—Mind-box limitation. Predicting the future based on past results.

—Thinking based on feelings. How you feel about something is a very unreliable way to live your life.

3. Everyone thinks I am incompetent.

—Taking things personally.

—No one knows how you feel. You cannot know what people are thinking.

—Routine pattern thinking. Getting so caught up in the expediency of the days that you don't notice compliments. Letting routine and old thinking patterns govern your life.

4. Someone cut in front of me in the line. They are disrespectful.

—Exaggerated/dramatic thinking

—The person may not have seen you and merely stepped into the line.

—Taking things personally.

It is hard to base an action, maybe as inadvertent as this, as being directed personally at you. Other people are living their daily lives, often operating on subconscious decisions.

5. I am not motivated to do anything. I must be a lazy person.

—Thinking based on feelings.

—When a person embraces a wide statement like this, they are basing it on how they feel about something.

—Routine pattern thinking.

This is an example of a person with a habitual pattern of thinking. This prevents them from seeing the bigger picture, as a lot of good may be being sown that will produce future fruit in their lives. This is divine destiny being constricted and edited by a habit of small thoughts.

6. *I should have bought a house this year instead of investing in gold. I should have known that gold will drop in price.*

—The "should have/would have" syndrome is predominant with this line of thinking. It is not possible to know ahead of time exactly how world markets and values of things will be over time. Hindsight is one thing, but putting it into practical use is another. It would serve you much better to say to yourself "I wish I would have known; however, I made the decision I did and it will all work out in the test of time." To blame and make yourself wrong over something that has already happened makes absolutely no sense at all.

7. *When I walk my dog, it always becomes aggressive and causes a scene with other people's dogs. They are going to think*

that I am a bad steward, and that I have a horrible dog.

—Negative mind-dominance is the type of thinking that this encompasses. It is focusing on the thoughts other people may be having that would be negative. Unless someone tells you specifically, it is impossible to know exactly what he or she is thinking at any given time. If they are dog owners themselves, they may be sympathetic toward you, by realizing that you might be having challenges in this area of training with your dog.

—Taking things personally. It may well be that the other people are not giving it much thought, but in our own minds, we paint a picture that is personal.

Food for Thought

What predicated your negative thoughts? Do you think it is genetic? Your interpretation and mind-editing of previous life circumstances? If they are from an internal manifestation, do you think that you can change them? Yes or no?

Plan of Action

All false thought processes or negative thinking patterns have been formed through the focus on negative things. Write down all that you are grateful for in your life. Make an effort to think of every area, as it might present a challenge for some, as we have a propensity in our human nature to be ungrateful or negative. Do this exercise on a daily basis for 1 week. This will help you gain a conscious awareness of being thankful for things on a daily basis. Awareness is paramount in making changes to your thought process. The more that you practice this principle, the more thankful you will become for more things in your life. Keep this going until you can log 10 things each day that you can be grateful for.

Thought Process

In order to change the thinking process, it must be challenged in two ways: 1) to establish how negative moods and thoughts are predicated by negative thinking habits and 2) to raise awareness of the types of negative thoughts discussed in this chapter so that you can more effectively challenge them.

As an example, I will use the following scenario: A husband shouted at his wife and is feeling depressed as a result.

Trigger or Objective Event: Shouted at His Wife

The trigger or objective situation is listed without any mind-box editing. It is independent of any negative thoughts attached to the event. It is important to separate thoughts and feelings from the event. For example, a person is walking a dog and thinking that everyone is disapproving of the dog when it barks loudly. It can be uncomfortable to think others are disapproving, but there is most probably a negative thought process in the person before the event occurred. The actual fact might be that the people are not at all disapproving, but instead would be sympathetic, as they also have a dog. This is a very different situation than the person has interpreted.

By the same token, note that the above event states the word "shouted" at his wife. The word "shouted" brings with it some element of mind-boxing and interpretation. How loud was his voice? Was it in the context of a discussion? Most husbands may have raised their voices at some point in a long marriage. Let us therefore accept that it was an accurate reflection of the trigger or objective event.

The husband notes how he felt at this time.

Automatic Negative Thought: Depressed; failure as a husband.

No new revelation thus far, just going off what happened. Let's look at how he felt? And what was his belief at the time it happened?

I am a failure as a husband.

I am like my dad.

I am fearful my wife will leave me.

This clarifies the fact that the husband became depressed. What was the conduit between the event and the feelings of depression? He was caught up in the "I." I am like my dad. I am a failure as a husband. I am fearful my wife will leave me. There may be other negative thoughts too. It is best to focus on the predominant ones initially, as they are the ones that have control over the mind.

Trigger or Objective Event: Shouted at His Wife
Automatic Negative Thought: I am a failure as a husband. I am like my father; he was always shouting. I am fearful my wife will leave me.
Negative Impact: Depressed; feels a failure as a husband
Realistic/Rational Thought: One event does not make me a failure. I do a lot of good, such as listen, take her on trips, and show care.

This sets the stage to challenge negative thought patterns and habits. It would give clarity to avoid thoughts about how his wife may, or may not, see him. It is important in reducing negative thinking to put the focus on (ANT), or automatic negative thinking. To recap their significance in the quality of our lives, we have approximately 60,000 thoughts per day, with 90 percent of those repeated, out of which 85 percent are negative. So it's easy to see how, without an awareness, our minds can become contaminated. When you gain an awareness of how this impacts your daily life, you can lift the falseness that has led to depression and a life far less than you were created to live.

Personalizing into Your Life

Write down in the column below a negative event in your life that you have experienced. In the first section, the trigger event, then your ANT response to it in the second section, the consequences or how you reacted in the third, and in the fourth, write down the realistic/rational thoughts that you can think of toward the event.

Trigger or Objective Event:
Automatic Negative Thought:
Negative Impact:

Realistic/ Rational Thought:

Preparing for Stress

The best way to be prepared to go into battle is to be equipped. As you have already learned, the battle is not the event, but instead in the mind. So it is beneficial to develop a strategy to cope with stressful events before they occur. Most folks wait for a storm to develop and then start to deal with it, rather than being prepared before it begins. It is in the words we use that can bring life or death to a situation. We can change the course of a potential stressor, or stressful situation, just by using the words that we use. By being aware of this and making a deliberate choice to use different words, we can soon find ourselves coping and not getting ruled by an event. We start to become the change in the circumstance rather than the circumstance becoming the change in us.

Being prepared is especially advantageous in dealing with situations that reoccur in your life as stress. This could be in bringing an idea to your boss, public speaking, flying, or going to the top of a high building. The basic steps for this are: 1) preparing for a stressful situation, 2) minimizing it as it begins to occur, 3) learning from the event so it doesn't have an impact should it reoccur.

Preparing for a Stressful Situation

Getting the mind right is the best defense for being in the right place to handle potentially stressful situations when they arise. Being able to deal with them doesn't happen during the event, but rather in being better prepared before, as if we can conquer them before, we can conquer them during. The best way to build our resistance is to build our abilities. An event or circumstance is only seen as a stressor if it is perceived that the event or circumstance is greater than our ability to handle it successfully.

As words can bring life or death, the most powerful thing you can use are positive affirmations against them. Positive affirmations are words and phrases to build and nurture your might and abilities.

—Greater is He in me than in this world.

—I can handle it.

—I will not get stressed, as I will get through it.

—No weapon fashioned against me shall prosper.

—If I couldn't handle it, it wouldn't be in my life.

—I am able to do all things in Christ, who strengthens me.

—I will not listen to any negative thinking.

—What has happened before is irrelevant to what is happening now.

—I will do great no matter what.

—The only problems are the ones that I permit in my mind.

The idea behind this exercise is to embrace a new way of coping with stress. It translates into you controlling the stressor instead of the stressor controlling you. Most of us, if we are not aware, are controlled by the ebbs and flows of life, rather than us taking charge of the situations we encounter and in so realizing that they can all work together for our good.

Even though stress is trying to control the things that you cannot, it will always be a part of human nature. This is mainly because of the effect of conditioning by society, media, and culture, and also our innate nature, which is born in separation of God. The key element to productive and effective living is to contain and minimize your reaction to stress.

In the awareness that some degree of stress will be a part of your life, you can then be prepared for it and begin to use some coping strategies. I will give you some NLP words (neuro-linguistic programming) that will bring life to resolution, and not feed the fire.

—I am greater than what is drawing up against me.

—I am a victor and not a victim.

—I will do what needs to be done.

—To get through it, I've got to first go through it.

—I will do things one step at a time.

—I will not be overwhelmed.

—This is just a chapter in my life.

—It's happening as it's supposed to be happening.

—I am equipped, as otherwise it would not be happening.

—I am not alone, as I am with God and nothing can work against me.

"Neuro-linguistic programming (NLP) is an approach to communication, personal development, and psychotherapy created by Richard Bandler and John Grinder in California in the 1970s. Its creators claim a connection between the neurological processes ('neuro'), language ('linguistic') and behavioral patterns learned through experience ('programming') and that these can be changed to achieve specific goals in life." (Cited taniasstudio.co.za)

The concept is basically that the words you use on a regular basis create your life. So negative words will give you a stress-filled, negative life, while positive words a positive, less stressful life. Words are powerful and can permeate the heart in a beneficial or detrimental way.

"Bandler and Grinder claim that the skills of exceptional people can be 'modeled' using NLP methodology, then those skills can be acquired by anyone. Bandler and Grinder also claim that NLP can treat problems such as phobias, depression, habit disorders, psychosomatic illnesses, myopia, allergies, common colds, and learning disorders, often in a single session. NLP has been adopted by some hypnotherapists and in seminars marketed to business and government." (Cited rodneywarren.com)

To put it simply, NLP takes the way the brain works and improves the way that you use it, and at the same time gives you a better life.

Each day, as a part of the cosmos, we experience noises, traffic, interactions with people, and our everyday functioning in life. All of these external events and occurrences run through the internal filters of the brain. This effectively becomes akin to a coffee filter in your home coffee maker, with all the experiences of your daily life going through the internal mechanism of your brain. What happens on the outside is what is left on the inside. This then becomes your emotional and psychological state. Depending on what we have filtered, this can be positive or negative. The quality of our mental states is in what we have given permission to filter in.

A given state is the result of the combination of an internal representation and a physiology. All that we do comes through a sensory system or input channel. This is made up of our 5 senses.

Sight: What we see and how we interpret those things

Hearing: What our ears hear and how we interpret it

Taste: What we taste and how we interpret it

Smell: What we smell and how we interpret it

Touch: What we touch and our interpretation through feel or texture

"The external event comes in through our sensory input channels and it is filtered and we process the event. As we process the event, we delete, distort and generalize the information that comes in, according to any number of several elements that filter our perception. In summary, NLP uses the language of the mind to consistently achieve our specific and desired outcomes." (Cited lifebeyondlimits.com.au)

Picture Your Way to Mental Health

1. Select a picture from your memory that, when you look at it, makes you feel good. Focus on the positive feelings.

2. Zoom the picture in to make it bigger and closer. Focus on how your feelings have changed or if they have changed.

3. Now zoom the picture out at the same time as dimming your thoughts. How do you feel? More or less positive?

When the picture is brighter, bigger, and nearer, most people respond in a more positive way. When the picture is dimmer and smaller, most people respond in a more negative way.

There is a close parallel between the way depressed people look at their lives and what they put their focus on. Depressed individuals look at good memories as distant, dim, and far away. Positive people focus on the brighter and bigger picture, with the memories close by. It's this focus that can impact lives and make a profound difference. Since our internal focus manifests all that is around us, it's within a change of an internal focus that can become the external revelation. When we change the way we see things, the things we see change. The sum total of the quality of our lives comes from what we focus our eyes and ears upon.

Dealing with the Accuser

How is your inner voice? We all have one. One that talks to us during our quiet or alone times. It can be a nagging voice or one that reminds us of our failings, shortcomings, inabilities, and lacking, things that have gone wrong, or might go wrong in the future. It's not our friend, but instead a harsh foe that criticizes and tries to discourage us at each and every opportunity. However, we spend so much time with it, that it becomes very often the main influencer in our lives. By changing the inner voice that we listen to, we can dramatically improve the quality of our lives.

1. What inner voices do you hear? One or more?

2. Take note if the voices are harsh or kind.

3. How does the voice make you feel, good or bad?

4. When is the voice triggered?

When you hear a negative voice, respond with a positive affirmation. For example, "You look lousy." Response: "I am fearfully and wonderfully made. A masterpiece created by God." "I never do well or get anywhere in life." Response: "I am very able to do all things well and bring to pass all things in my path." "They are not going to think I am any good."

Response: "I will not listen to others, but instead listen to what God says about me. I am fearfully and wonderfully made and created to do great exploits for a time just like this."

As you can see, it is about not letting the inner voice or accuser have its way. The accuser is a liar and seeks to kill and destroy your life. By becoming aware, you can help distinguish it before it takes a hold of your mind with its false reality. You can change your life by changing your inner voice, as when you change from within, you also change from without. When your inner voice is calm, loving, and supportive, your life will take on a whole new and better quality. It's all about getting to know our individual inner mechanism, and then making changes to have the life that we were meant to lead. In embracing that NLP is the language of the mind, we can change our lives through retraining the mind to speak a different language.

CHAPTER SIX

Dealing with the Limbic Mind

This part of your mind is foremost in controlling your everyday life. It does all the functions we want it to do, without us making a conscious effort. I am going to take a really good look at it with you, and the way that it all started.

To explain it this way, when a pilot is flying a plane, he is making a conscious effort to be at the right nautical speed and direction, but when it is in autopilot, the plane is flying within preset parameters without the need for conscious adjustment. The way this all started in us is through our childhoods, the things that we have been exposed to, whether societal or experiential, have all left a unique imprint in the way that we react and make the decisions we do in our lives today.

Both our positive and negative experiences are stored in our bodies. These then impact every neural cell in our bodies. This is why, when we feel stressed or anxious, we can experience stomachaches, headaches, stiff necks and restricted breathing. Every thought that we have or will have will have a reaction. As humans, most of our thoughts are negative. In actual fact, 85 percent. Those single thoughts are not detrimental, but as they pool together and gather, they build in our neuropeptide receptors, which run throughout the entire body. This process acts like a bank account, so what you put in grows as you continue to make deposits. Unless checked on a regular basis, we can end up being a negative and toxic person, as all emotions are constantly being processed by the body.

What we see with our eyes and what we hear with our ears becomes our reality. For example, if during my childhood I was told that taking a motorboat to sea is dangerous, that thought is then manifested in my mind each time I take a motorboat to sea. The limbic mind reacts in this emotional way to something in the present, usually from the past. It is not seeing something the way it is. Of course, a motorboat can be dangerous if the seas are rough, the boat is not maintained well, or is in inexperienced hands. The thing itself cannot be dangerous. A car is not dangerous. A plane is not dangerous. Drinking wine is not dangerous, but it is what is done around it, that can create a dangerous situation. That applies to anything we do in life.

Another example is that we had a spell of really warm weather with little rainfall. Immediately when you comment to people, "Oh, the weather is great," they reply with, "We need rain." This is the limbic mind, which is programmed to react to something in the present. Of course rain comes. It has been raining for 6,000 years.

When we slip into that mind-set, it really takes control of our minds, by putting them on cruise control. That is really what runs our minds. The cruise control, limbic episodes happen in all areas of life. It could be leaving the office while thinking, "Well, someone is going to put a lot of work on my shoulders. I am going to be rushed/stressed and not able to do it." This is a negative way of dealing with things, by mind-boxing from a program set from our past.

Most of us are not aware of why we are thinking the way we are thinking. We have done it for so long, that it has become our automatic, (autopilot) way of thinking. It obviously puts tremendous restrictions on our lives. Even though we are moving forward, we are not really open to seeing things the way they truly are. The mind and body are wonderfully intertwined, and interact to the environment around us.

This is sensory living. What we see, smell, taste, hear and touch. This can involve pleasurable experiences like petting a dog, or painful experiences such as being beaten as a child. Each experience we have leaves a deposit or imprint. The more senses used, the greater and longer lasting the imprint. Traumatic or abusive experiences can leave physical and emotional imprints that last a lifetime if not resolved.

So Great ... But How Can I Do It?

It's easier to forgive than to live in a state of unforgiving. The work it takes may be hard, but living in a state of pain and sadness is much harder. The limbic mind is an internal manifestation of our external revelation. It's the outer having dominion over the inner. This very often means that we are reacting to something from an inner emotive trigger, that is stored deeply within us from our past experiences and our mind-editing of them. It can be words used over us by another, or smells that we encounter, as they all play a part in how we react. It's a dance between outer and inner self. The outer moving and positioning the inner. Like a microwave, it's the inner force that has the ultimate effect over the outer condition. The dance can be good, like entering a room that has the sweet smell of a cake, as this can trigger memories of happy, joyous family gatherings. Or this could work the other way, by rekindling childhood memories and the abuse associated therein. Each day is a blank, glorious canvas; however, the memories we have and our automatic emotional triggers to those, can have a powerful effect on what we paint on it. Pleasant memories give us light, unpleasant ones paint dark colors. If these thoughts are not dealt with, they can lead you to have a miserable life. (Please see Chapter 7, The Heart Is like a Bank Account.)

Free Me of Limbic Captivity

Your experiences have all left an imprint on you, which has been stored deeply in every cell of your body. "Let me free," I hear you say … We're going to do this. There needs to be a tearing down of some of the things that have grown a wall in your heart. You are now in a corridor, with a key to a door. The door can open you up to everything or set you back into limitation set by years of imprinting. To be able to step into the door of everything requires awareness, acceptance, forgiveness, and a conviction to work through things that will, at times, bring discomfort.

Within gaining an awareness, things become much clearer. You have a lot more clarity in decision-making. In order to change the imprint and your way of thinking, you have to go into a process that will initiate a deliberate mind-set change. You have to connect to the awareness of what you are doing now, and accept that it is not serving you. This will then open a channel to rewire your system, with a different thought pattern. By changing brushes, using different colors, you will then get a different result on the canvas of your life.

Through creating a oneness with all that is in this very moment, you create the ability to stay present. Neither in the past nor in the future. The reason some of us stay in the past or future is that all of the pain is in the present. So we stay in the past, or we stay in the future. It is a learned way of coping. A coping mechanism.

Developing an awareness of why you think the way you think is the key to being able to change. So when we deliberately change our minds, the conscious mind will eventually become the rewired subconscious. This is the limbic mind. Through a higher consciousness, you will change the way you think. You will change the way you do things. The payoff for that is, your autopilot will be a new way of thinking. As the limbic emotional system is wired to the prefrontal cortex, which is responsible for critical thinking, both require to be meshed together to make a paradigm change.

This will predicate a predominance of positive thinking, as it will have minimized the old negative paradigms. This is why you get positive and negative people. Positive people are looking at things through a positive imprint, as that has become their limbic way of operating. Negative people, who are the majority, unfortunately, are looking through what has happened before and how that may affect the future. This is keeping their present and future in a veil of limitations.

Alchemy for Change

The world offers change in terms of the seeing eye. There emanates the quote, "See it to believe it." These touted solutions can come in many guises: the therapist, Dr. Phil, Oprah, antidepressants, overspending, over-drinking, compulsive relationships, and any other addictive behaviors. These are self-sustaining through the serotonin hormones released by the repetition of the behavior itself. (Please see Chapter 4, Habits.)

I am not going to use this chapter to judge healing modalities, as I would not want to attempt to convince you otherwise of what you have decided to accept in your own free will. I will instead choose to enlighten and inform better. My hope is that you would then gain a clearer picture so that you can decide for yourself. The only lasting decisions are the ones made on our free will and then sustained by conviction.

If worldly choices did offer a solution, it would be evident in a measurable change in human behavior. The reality is that all around, we can evidence an increase in despair, anger, hopelessness, and interracial animosity of globally significant proportions. The level ground for all people is finding a solution to how they feel deep in their inner beings. A solution to the "agree to disagree" state of the world. The problem is not in lack of abundance, knowledge, talent, or resources. The brilliant hack of Sony pictures through the exploitation of servers all over the world in an attempt to hide its origin. AirPenguin was developed in 2009 by a German company. It's a mechanical penguin robot that can navigate cramped spaces underwater and can also fly. It is intended to extract research tool samples deep from the seabed. There are even inventions that covert moisture from soil evaporation and return it underground for conversion into water for crops.

All this in an attempt to create more significance and the world a better place? Apparently not! The answer is not in more, but in seeing more of what is already present. The present is a gift; that is why it is referred to as the "present." The solution is in finding better hearts, to bring about more love. This will bring a solution to the world's biggest mystery, which is how to find peace, as we can all determine the "more" is obviously not working. Now let me take you on a journey toward a better life.

The Solution Is in Going Back, Not Forward

There are two basic struggles in humanity moving forward: 1) forgiving ourselves for what we have perceived to have done to others and 2) forgiving others for what we have perceived they have done to us. This manifests in our rational need to forgive others for their words or actions over us, or needing to forgive ourselves for our actions that may have caused hurt to others. The irrational: on the one hand, we hold ourselves responsible for pain that others have caused us, and on the other, we feel guilty for pain we may have been a part of causing others even though we could do nothing to change the situation and did not intentionally cause pain.

I am not going to theologize or use pride to bring my slant, as that's what many do to get their niche. We end up with no solutions, but a whole world of self appointed "leaders" trying to get their "knowledge" out there. It becomes a world of interpretations without solutions. This is evidenced by what we now have all around us. Let's not walk around in a circle, but instead wash our pride away, and accept we need intercession. Intersession is progression, while pride remains smoke and mirrors to no solution at all. Let's remain open to change, as what we have presently is not presently working. It's in finding Light that becomes a world solution. It's the Light of Christ, having emanated from eternity through God, the Father. God is love in its purest form, and The Creator of All things. Christ became God in the flesh. He took on the power and the likeness of God; therefore, the pure love and light in God became manifest in Christ the Son. This was to act as a bridge to mankind to bring Unity from its separation. The third part of the Trinity, referred to as The Holy Spirit, is the combustion that brings the Light in and through you. In other words, The Father is the Divine spirit, the essential Light, the Light then having become manifest in Christ, with the conductor for change being the Holy Spirit. No change can happen without a willingness of humanity to surrender and let the Spirit correct them by a cleansing process. This is not being judged, so please don't shut down, but instead let the love guide you back to your original form and intention. No light can be present in our lives, without the source from where it sprang.

This is evidenced by the visible, the creation all around: the sun, mountains, oceans, and deserts, and all visible living forms within. The water was first, and made alive by the Spirit. There was darkness that became Light by The Word of God, the beginning of all things. This means that by alchemy that it can be made tangible and visible. However, it is the Spirit, which is the invisible state that makes it all visible. To sum this up, the source of everything is God, the Light is Jesus, and the transcending power is The Holy Spirit.

As everything is connected, let me pose this to you … It's our disconnectedness that brings about the chaos we find in ourselves and in the world in general today. God brings Cosmos out of chaos. This is a complex and orderly system, known as The Universe. The Universe is a spiritual Light. It is important to remember that we are spiritual beings having a human (corporeal) bodily moment here on earth. To transform and transcend time, we need to connect back to the source (God). The time and space we associate with our lives, are a false you, a temporary illusion within our bodily Being. Time and space don't exist, as eternity is not the perpetuity of time, as in eternity, time does not exist. Time and space is a human mind-box, as in eternity, time and space doesn't exist. It is not possible to measure a year, two years, or two hundred years, as there is no reference point to either. The utterances of our active mind label and restrict us to live a life of judgment and limitations. By prayer and developing a personal relationship with God, you move from temporal to eternal. You move away from the noise to the stillness of God. This paradigm shift can be life changing. For more introspection, see Chapter 3, The Power of Thoughts.

CHAPTER SEVEN

The Heart is Like a Bank Account

When we are born, we start off completely from scratch with no previous experiences, no previous heartbreaks, and no previous disappointments. As we go through life, what happens is that the heart is akin to a bank account. Every experience we edit in our minds as being good or bad, we actually put back into our heart as a deposit. Before long, it becomes tainted. This is caused by making transfers, which are actually transferred mostly from our negative mind.

So the mind becomes a reservoir that pushes out into the

heart. Experiences come in many different shapes and sizes. It could be personal experiences from relationships. It could be experiences from words that have been said over us by parents, by siblings, by peers at school, by teachers, interactions with adults, interactions with people at work, relational ones, non-relational ones, just people we encounter in stores and on streets. All of these things gather in the heart. Without transformation, we remain on a journey of not getting better as a person, but more and more bitter. Be become more closed to new opportunity as a result.

In terms of experiences and life events, we gather usually the negative ones because that is how society is geared by the media and accepted paradigms. Most of us are conditioned to focus on negative things through a limited mind-set that we have embraced. The abundance mind-set would be one of infinite possibility, unrestricted by limitations. These limitations are man-made, as we were not born that way. We took it as being our truth and therefore live that way. The abundance of our Creator is one of pure love. That can only bring positivity to the table. So the purer our hearts, the more positive our outlook. To have a different outlook, we must first change our "inlook." It is the battle of light and dark.

It is the darkness of this world that labels things as being bad or negative. This pushes those mind-sets upon us, which we then permit to steal and destroy our Light. This then becomes what we mold our life to, our paradigm. If we view all interactions as going into this bank account, what happens is we get a lot of buildup. If these things are not dealt with, what's the result? We get overflow, overflow of negativity. That affects us in terms of how we see ourselves, and how we see ourselves will be how we see other people. If we put a label on someone else and voice their limitations, that is a reflection of what we are feeling from within. What we see around is what we see from within. The limitations and restrictions are not because what is around us is that way; it's the way we are, and hence what our surroundings have become to us.

It can only be through changing perspective that we can see the things that we have encountered differently. So we have to look back at all these things that have molded and shaped us over many years. Go back into this bank account, and like an ATM card, take out the negative deposits one by one.

If it is words people have spoken over us, we need to come to the revelation that they spoke from their own set of limitations and mind-sets, and put those upon us. What we have, in effect, done is given them permission to put those upon us. We have taken them on as being fact or truth about us. We have a belief system that is being founded upon what we have heard about ourselves. Our mind has edited in our mind-box in terms of what has been said.

Very simply, you can say the same thing to two different people. One person takes it a completely different way than the other. It is not just the spoken word, but how we view the spoken word. How we personally edit and store in our minds, will then permeate into our hearts. It is neither the words nor the circumstances that have impacted our hearts, but how we have stored them.

We are walking around with all of these past experiences, and from those, our interpretations and perspectives, which are mostly channeled through negative thoughts. How do we think the condition of our hearts is by now? We have the ability to store more positive thoughts, but that has to be a deliberate action. We have two parts of the mind that are foremost in our mind-editing system: the prefrontal cortex, which is the logical mind, and the limbic mind, which is the autopilot, emotional mind. The mind that sources all of the negative is the limbic mind, as with it, we react with our emotions and feelings. It is these emotions and our feelings that impact and taint our hearts. To make a change, what needs to take place is a consistent, conscious, deliberate effort to raise our awareness to be sure we edit things in a positive way. When re-channeling those on a consistent basis, it will lead to a rewiring of the limbic mind. This emotional mind, which is the autopilot, where we react from, will become more positive as we continue to clean out the bad debt in our bank account (heart). As we react from our autopilot mind, our instinctive reactions will become more positive. This will change you and also be the change that you would like to see in others around you.

To change that autopilot mind, in other words, to change the way we are living out our lives on a daily basis, we need to be aware of what we are putting away. For example, this is a simple one ... if someone says, "Look, you are not going to be good at doing this." Rather than take offense, or taking that onboard and storing it in that negative bank, we can develop a positive dialogue with ourselves. "Well, okay, I notice that the person has made this comment." They are entitled to their own opinion; however, I am not going to wear this as a badge. I am not going to put this into my heart. I am not going to accept this as being a true image of me. The person is operating from his or her own limitation, and I am not aware of his or her past, to accept that their view is accurate of me in the present. Most people, unless they have been on a course of heart correction, project their fears and limitations on you. This is referred to as mirroring. They are reflecting their inner condition on you.

What I will look to is what God says. "You are fearful and wonderfully made. Grace in you. The same spirit that conquered death lives inside of you." So very simply, we need to take onboard what is being said by the source, not by an interpreted version from another human being.

A cleansing system of the human heart stores things as a bank account. Very simply, the ATM would be taking those out, which would be the prefrontal cortex (the logical mind), channeling, and not putting those into the limbic mind. We can change our lives dramatically by removing what is already in our bank accounts, and stored in our emotional minds (limbic), and replacing that with things that would serve us way better. Words that would build and not break down. For example, "I am not a victim, but I am a conqueror." "I am not unwanted or worthless, but I am loved by God and created for His divine plan and purpose for my life." "I am not all alone, as He is always with me." "I am not abandoned, as He will never leave or forsake me." "I am not an addict, as this is a temporary season, and He will heal me." "I am not broke, but I am getting ready to birth new ground." These are just some of the hundreds of self-affirmations you can use to drown out your inner voice (enemy).

We can reprogram our minds to the way they were originally created to be, in much the same way it was done to get them to their current state, before our analytical minds took onboard the things spoken over us and our interpretations of events as being truth. These then got stored in our limbic mind (emotional), which then becomes very much how we live our lives out on a daily basis. We are not consciously thinking through things all the time. We are reacting to things, and this comes through our false self.

By developing an awareness of this human heart bank account, we can begin to make deposits and withdrawals. We can channel those and use an ATM system to take those out (withdrawals). The new ones coming in (deposits) will be conscious decisions by the conscious mind (prefrontal cortex), to put away positive stored feedback.

All negative thoughts are a perspective of what is. What is is glorious, what is is great. Your perspective is your mental view or outlook. As human beings, our perspective is often askew, coming from our past experiences and taken on beliefs. We cannot possibly view the present and the future negatively if it were not for the past. In order to make a change, we need to rework that system and channel positive things. Many of us are so adjusted to the patterns of this world, that we are overdrawn on negative thoughts and do not even realize it. We need to break some things off so that we can rebuild.

In order to make a change to the words spoken over us or negative perceptions we have taken onboard as being truth, we have to rework and rewire them by gaining an awareness of where they came from. It is from an assumption from others, through their disappointments, failures, setbacks, and out of those, their limitations, that we have then given permission to have them placed upon us, and accept them as a being our limitations. In our minds, these then manifest as being our disappointments. A disappointment can be edited as a growth potential. For example, if your employer "lets you go" to reduce salary costs, you have lost that job, but if you dwell on the loss and not on the new opportunity of being able to move forward, you will be on a downward, exponential spiral. You will be magnifying the loss and taking that onboard rather than the potential of moving on. A setback is a setup for greater things to come into your life.

When one door closes, a better opportunity opens. If you were meant to have that opportunity, the door would not have closed. It closes to move you forward in the Master Plan and purpose for your life. So any setback is an opportunity for growth, not for being put back. We must be very conscious in developing that through our conscious mind. We are then not preparing ourselves for a setback or a put-back or a drop-back. We need to really embrace all of this. The Word says to guard our hearts with all diligence, as out of it flow all the issues of life. This means that we have stewardship of our hearts but must be careful what we allow to go in, as everything we do flows from it. Yet, the heart is deceitful and desperately wicked, and because we are all so easily influenced by the world around us, our hearts need guarding. We reduce so God can then increase.

It's the same thing with a relationship; if somebody says they no longer want to be with you, rather than dwelling on the loss, let us dwell on the great times we had or even the challenges we faced (growth opportunities). "Those experiences were great; however, this is not the plan for me, because I am being shifted to be in a position to be open to new things." This approach turns setbacks into an opportunity to be open to newness. We can change hearts by how we look at things, so then what we see becomes different. The microwave system, meaning from inside/out. We can change perspective and change vision. We can take away the ruin in our life and build glory: moving forward, gaining strength, gaining wisdom, gaining endurance, and also gaining the potential for a life far greater. Let's see things through a higher manifestation, a clearer perspective, by shifting paradigms to break molds and break free to a brand-new life. This all has to be done by a conscious, consistent effort by the prefrontal cortex. This is the part of our brain that orchestrates our actions in accordance with our internal goals.

The Power of Forgiveness

In our carnal state, forgiveness needs to be worked to be attained. It's one of the most powerful things that you will ever be able to do ... so pay special attention to these next few sentences, please. Forgiveness is a deliberate action. Forgiveness is a choice. It is the act of compassionately releasing the desire to punish, avenge, or hold a grudge against another person for an offense that YOU have CHOSEN to take personally. By making the choice to forgive, you disempower the other person from having control of your emotions. To live in a state of unforgiving is to give the other person/persons dominion over your heart. Very simply, to live in a state of unforgiving is harder in the long run than learning how to forgive. Resolution of the past is solution to the present.

To attain higher level living, we must develop the aroma of God's heart. It is from that basis that you can build the grace from within, to be able to handle challenges from others at a higher level. Let me explain it this way, of course if someone betrays, insults, or hits you, it's natural to feel angry. It is an instinctive human reaction to respond in the same fashion. It's fine to have anger, as first you must feel anger in order to forgive.

Even though it is natural to feel vengeful as you want to get even, or give hurt back, by doing so, you become your worst self. You go down to the same level as the person you judge and abhor. A wrong with a wrong becomes a war. The wrong that you are trying to right will be antithetical to ever finding peace. This would be like a guest spilling wine on your carpet and you responding by spilling some more. A life of revenge, grudges, and any type of ill feelings is diametrical opposite to the path you are trying to connect to. You want peace, and you are only creating war for yourself. For all you know, the other person is probably not giving you a second thought. The best way to nullify any actions or words used against you, is to not give them dominion over you. You got it—don't react!

There are some very real abuses and injustices that we encounter in the course of just everyday living. Yes, your father verbally abused you. Yes, your wife had an affair with a friend of yours. Yes, you found out that you lost your job as a result of others' wrongful gossip. These are all very real, and if not dealt with at a higher level, they become potentially heart-changing experiences. If not dealt with in a different way than the tools of our human nature, we are in for a very rough time. We need to gather tools of peace to create peace, as the tools of war will only bring the fruits of more!

These images and beliefs literally reverberate through the cells of our entire bodies, influencing how we feel, how we act, our relationships, our success, and even our overall health.

Jesus said it was out of the heart that the mouth speaks. Elsewhere in the Bible, it talks about the need for a transformation. "Transformation is needed not just for the mind but for the heart." (Cited letusreason.org) Transformation is a complete or major change in someone's, or something's appearance.

To heal and become a whole person, we need to begin by healing the heart, as the heart is our estuary and all things flow out of it. The heart we have today needs healing and protecting. I refer to "the heart we have today," as this is not the condition of the one we were born with, but the one we have developed by the editing of the sum total of our life experiences.

The heart is like an estuary, as all things flow out of it. It is so important to get this, as it can enhance your health, relationships, and your life's accomplishments.

Sounds Great, but How Can I Do It?

It is paramount to realize that the person doing the abusing, in word or in act, is mirroring the broken state that they are feeling from deep within themselves. They are displaying an external manifestation of an internal condition. They have internal damage from their past hurts and heartbreaks. Please do not label this on others as the societal norms do, which is "mental." Indeed, maybe some have mental disorders, but most are just plain hurt … toxic hearts. They are victims and not victors in their stories. We all begin with a blank canvas. It is then born out of the choices we make, from our individual circumstances that ultimately mold and determine how the picture we paint on our canvas becomes.

For example, when a husband abuses his wife, it is most likely that he has experienced instability, hostility of words or actions between, or by one or both parents or guardians. This has been his environment or influence, so he is mirroring this as a result of his childhood conditioning. The environment we are in becomes the conditioning or aroma we display. Like a sponge absorbs what is around it, so do we.

For example, if your father left you and your mother when you were very young, it's most likely you suffer from abandonment issues, with or without realizing it. This then manifests in you seeking value and acceptance from relationships. The people you choose, or are likely to target, are the ones who will keep one leg in and one leg out. This means that they will not be in a place to give you full commitment, be it from their past circumstances or emotional health point. This creates a cycle of they get what they want, they leave, you then get into another relationship, they get what they want, they leave, and this is how the story goes on and on.

To make a change requires a shifting. This is when something moves from one quality to another. The heart would be restored from its present condition, to its former condition. This sounds good, but how can I have my original heart back?

Getting in Touch with Your Core Self

As our minds compete with the clutter and noise of the routine of our day, we need to hush things down to a level where we can pay attention to how we feel. Attention doesn't require us to think more, but rather less. If we get into a state of thinking less, we will be able to get into a state of feeling more. Remember, how we act out in our everyday lives is through our emotional state. When we connect to our feelings, we can get deep into our inner-self, because the obstruction of thoughts has been removed to give us clear passage to our core. The core is the central part of the heart, the estuary that flows like a stream into our every cell. It is the throne of life and emotions.

When you feel things around you and your attention is now focused, what do you feel? Is it anger? Is it fear? Is it sadness? There may be other peripheral feelings such as heaviness, uneasiness, or tiredness. It's not important for you to label them, as this will move you into a place of mind-editing (false self). What's more important is identifying how you feel and bringing that into your awareness. This will bring you into a state of consciousness, which will light the path for you to be able to recognize your true feelings. It's in this state of recognition that you can begin to identify the canvas that you have painted into your heart. Being out of thoughts and into feelings will create acceptance, which is key to healing. Without acceptance, there can only be denial. In the entirety of the organism of the body, a single emotion has a short shelf-life. It is when, in our thoughts (head) that these emotions accumulate, gathering like mold on the inside of a wall. It is out of years of multiplying that they surface as our pain body. Without correction, these will give you a toxic heart, a cynical mind, limitations, anger, self-loathing, the tendency to be critical of others, and make for a miserable life.

In connecting to the awareness of our feelings at a deeper level, we can manifest forgiveness toward ourselves or another person, past, present, or in the future. You may ask "How can I not forgive the future?" This is our mind refusing to accept change and our inability to control it. When you remain in a state of unforgiving, you are not in control, as you have submitted control to the person or circumstance that keeps you in that bondage. Forgiveness is in releasing the grief or grievance against a person/persons, and in doing so, taking control over how you feel away from them. Very simply, YOU are now in control. The only thing that not forgiving can do is feed your ego and allow your false self to continue in its perpetuity. The mind by itself cannot forgive, only the heart can. Making the paradigm shift of turning anger to forgiveness is actually making anger work for you, as opposed to against you. That is why restoring the heart to its original quality is so fundamental in having a life that flows through you, instead of a constant state of resistance and stagnation.

How to Get Your Original Heart Back

"Life is full of pain and disappointments which bring sorrow and discouragement, so the heart needs to be cheered, comforted, and encouraged. But our tendency is to seek to cheer and comfort our hearts with the methods of the world—through our strategies for happiness, through the details of life as with the pursuit of power, pleasure, possessions, position, and the like. God has given us all things to enjoy, but God's plan for lasting joy and encouragement comes from a heart that has been prepared and fixed to trust the Lord (Jn. 16:27; Ps. 37:4)" (Cited internet source)

We spend a lifetime seeking something outside of ourselves to find "happiness," but all the time it's right in front of us. By that, I mean it can only be attained through our deep "inner person." We can bring happiness to a person, event, or a day, but a person, event, or a day can't bring it to us. It's a product of an internal revelation that then becomes an external manifestation. We can then take our happiness into any season in life, as we no longer need to attach to anything to "make us happy."

Is My Heart the Condition of My Life?

Actually your life is the condition of your heart. All our daily actions, what we say, do, and think mirror the condition of our hearts. This is why you need to guard your heart with all due diligence. This is because what we allow to settle will ultimately be what comes out. Let me explain it like this, if we take a new white shirt out of its box for the first time, we see the brilliant white splendor, and a virgin luster about it. Wear it for a day on Wall Street and then examine the collar. It's soiled as a result of the grime of the environment it has been exposed to. Our hearts are exactly the same! Without a divine revelation and illumination, they are on a course of getting soiled. Just in living out our lives, taking on paradigms from societal norms, and very often not being aware of a better way, makes us often times bitter and not better.

To get our original heart back requires a course correction. An evaluation for a restoration. Restoration denotes a shift, a change from one condition to a previous condition. From one quality to another quality. To renovate or restore, means there was something before. Something before our life experiences lied to us, and our hearts became tainted by the labels we permitted either by the words or actions of others to be placed on us. All of this together makes a big impact on the human heart. You only need to drive down any street to observe the selfish nature of many drivers. This is not how they were born, but instead how life has made them.

How Can I Be the Change That I Want to See in Others?

Please be open to what you are now about to read ... and if not, examine what you are feeling, as it's a heart issue that you have identified. I'm not judging but just being real.

God made everything out of nothing and created the heavens and the earth. He also created us in His image. Image denotes character, which is personality, nature, temperament, and representation.

The challenge begins in our innate nature, as human beings do not act or think the way God does. The world system is to build the "self." This can be through education, money, and ego. We have our own idea of success that we have been molded to think is the one we need to life up to. However, if you spend any time listening to the success concepts of the present day, you will become aware of two main fronts. Firstly, most of the media, self-help books, wellness seminars, conferences, motivational speakers, and the general paradigms of modern culture and its influences, focus on the extrinsic self—on how much we can gather, build ourselves up to become this super strong, bullet-proof independent individual. Seldom do you read or hear much on the intrinsic person, on the heart, the estuary of our thoughts, motives, ambitions, values, and decisions. And second, even when any emphasis is placed on heart issues, it is more focused on getting than giving. This is why the world is the way it is today: relationships at their lowest point, governments posturing, amazing species of animals going extinct, resources pushed over and beyond capacity. As God created you, He is the maker and He has the answers to all our problems, with the emphasis on heart. It is so fundamental in determining how we conduct our lives. For example, take a car you want to restore. Very naturally, you go to the manufacturer's handbook for direction.

To be very real, the main reason we all need a heart "oil change" is that in our pride, we build a resistance to go to our manufacturer (God). We then embark on a lifelong search for "happiness." We have allowed the world to put our thinking into its paradigm. So we then go on an adventure to search for a solution. Education. Make more money. Buying costly things to feel accomplished. Traveling to see if people are different, or to escape. Prozac because our therapist gets tired of our complaining. Self-help because we think the more we can build our egos, the more happy we will become. Motivational speakers tell us they will make us float like a butterfly and sting like a bee. All this to avoid the idea of accepting that we are not in control. To save you wasting anymore time searching for what you can have now … we are not!! I spent many years doing the same until the light started to illuminate the lies in 2006. Since then, I cannot put into words how I feel. Keep reading, please.

The questions we must now all ask ourselves are "Am I guarding my heart? Is it a priority?" These answers will determine its condition, and from that, the condition of our lives.

Even believers in their acceptance that there is an alternative to worldly paradigms, are at times veiled by the powerful influences of human nature, and its innateness to be wretched in pursuit of selfish gain, lust, and self-destruction. A great many of us, if we are really honest, don't really love ourselves, let alone love God and others. Our false self takes on a reality that we can live life independently from God. By putting pride aside, we unlock the door to the treasure chest of happiness; however, when we let the lies become our truth, we are robbed of the greatest treasure: happiness. It's free, and yet we spend our entire lives paying to find it. You can't buy it, work it, sex it, medicate it, or add anything to it, as the answer has been there yesterday, today, and forever. It's God!!! God is the potter and we are the clay.

To use biblical references, we can be:

1. People committed to building our own cisterns, but these always turn out to be broken cisterns that can hold no

water. (Jeremiah 2:3)

2. People who seek to walk by the light of our own man-made firebrands. (Isaiah 50:11)

In staying on readings in Isaiah, we can be influenced by many things from the north, south, east, and west, these being the world's paradigms for life, as opposed to God's Master Plan for each individual. This sets us on a path of getting rather than giving, resisting rather than flowing, struggle rather than peace.

This results in the paradigms of our lives becoming a "tug-of-war." The world and all its influences and ideals have us orchestrating our lives in the way we think that they should be, and God at the other end. It's not surprising why there is a world turned upside down by its inhabitants. Global monetary ideals shattered, families fragmented, races divided, nations and their people at war, character and ethics overlooked, with personal edification and achievement the goal.

What worked for me was turning from worldly influences, as this would not give me change, but created more of the same limited paradigms that got me seeking a change in the first place. I went to God, "The Heart Surgeon General." He created me so it was like going to the manufacturer's handbook. As we have established, a good deal of changing heart, and so being able to improve the quality of your life, is in the reduction of self (pride), so that you are open to finding something that might work better for you.

It is important to remember that all the pain and suffering we have endured is directly as a result of the words or actions of others. So we are called to step into something new, so that we can rise to new levels. Would we pour new wine into old wine skins? No, we would buy new wine skins. The heart, in the same way, needs new counsel to create new paradigms. This will not be putting a bandage on the old, but transforming the old to become a new way of thinking and living. Part of our false self is founded in our human nature, and the idea that we can do it alone and trust our solutions is spurred by a defense mechanism. When we think we can do it alone, we get prideful, arrogant, angry, and unable to change as our hearts become hardened. This can only result in a miserable life regardless of what we have or add to ourselves.

As you have read, the heart is, before anything else, the key player in influencing the quality of your life, and of those around you. Even Christians, or those yielded to a higher power, must engage in a regular heart assessment. This is because in the fast pace of modern life, with all the myriad of media, multicultural cities, and opinions pulling at our hearts, unless we are careful, we could be going way off track, even when thinking that we are doing "all the right things." We could be going to church or our place of worship for a lifetime, and in actuality it is nothing more than a routine, much like drinking our morning Starbucks. Unless, there is a deliberate choice, with a conviction to soften and change our hearts, we will remain nothing more than people with external religiosity. That's right, just a routine. It's not the time you spend doing something, but the change you make out of the time that you spend doing something that counts.

Unless we really deal with our hearts, our religious striving or our worship of God becomes egocentric. And though this, we can be purified and brought into the service of God through the Word. Too often true religion is corrupted and nullified by cravings and striving for self-centered concerns like power, comfort, and security. The Word of God is more than a handbook of doctrine and a set of prescriptions for proper living that we can apply to make life work out the way we want. It is a God-breathed book designed to involve us passionately with the living God so that we trust Him even when life doesn't seem to make sense. We don't need to keep trying to figure out all the hows and whys of life. All we can do is trust that God is in charge and that a good and Master Plan continues fully in place.

CHAPTER EIGHT

Looking in All Different Places

It is certain that we live in a consumer-oriented, materialistic, hedonistic society with the focus on personal gain. This has given rise to the idea of happiness being in personal success, acknowledgments, acceptance, material possessions, and creature comforts. We have taken on the mistaken worldly paradigm that if we just acquire certain things, then we can be truly happy and even secure. As a result, people develop their own protocols to get to where they think they need to be to live happily and fulfilled. Of course, these chosen protocols are very much the result of the mind-set of a media-driven, fear-based, God as a pluralistic, privatized, secular, or even agnostic lifestyle. With all these different paradigms vying for our acceptance, it's not without cause that there is more teenage suicide than at any previous time in history. Add to this anti-depressant use, sleep disorders, and general feelings of despair, making it really fundamental that we take a hard look at what is taking place at unacceptable and unprecedented levels.

So many of us are relentlessly searching for something to add meaning to ourselves. We are searching for meaning and purpose for our existence. A reason to be here in this world. This could be through work, groups that we join, sporting events, or relationships. We try to find meaning in relationships, so we go from one to another.

In order to become more aware, we need to go deeper within ourselves to see the things we have presently within our life, the things that we have around us, the people in our lives, opportunities, and grace. Then build gratitude and contentment for those things. It is important in doing so to become aware that you are a spirit Being, having a human moment. Our bodies are nothing more than a "container" for our spirit, body, and soul. It is in a state of disconnection to God (The Creator) of all things that predicates us to be struggling to find meaning and purpose for our lives. Within the realm of connectedness we intertwine with our purpose as it becomes revealed that we already have all we need to complete our personal journey. As you move forward within greater awareness you begin to see what you have differently, through new eyes bringing with them renewed hope and joy. In the way you were drinking what amounted to salt water before which meant that you needed more and more, you now find yourself quenched and satiated.

Finding Your Source

It is in connecting to God that your true Being can be met. We cannot look at God as a word, as we associate our false selves with words. This is because when we start to associate words or language to something it is our interpretation of those words that determine what the ultimate meaning of that word is. The word "God" can mean a great deal or very little, depending on how it is used. It has been misused in so many ways, over so many years in our human language. The mind is the greatest barrier in truly connecting to your source and therefore the true core you. In our minds, God can point to transcendental reality or an image that you have chosen to interpret. The word "God" is just a word, unless you have come to know what the word points to, or feel His presence at the center of your life. The word as a reference will keep God as something you need to attach to, as opposed to connect with in your Being. For example, take "wine" as a word. We mind-box and label what it might be like before we even taste it. This brings a context that is birth from our separation. When we associate logic or a meaning to a word in our humanity (separation), we cut ourselves off from experiencing the fullness or reality of what actually is. We cannot study Being, understand it, or comprehend it, as any association from our minds will create disassociation to God. To get closer requires a state of awareness that God is in you, has been in you since the beginning, and is not something you need to connect to from the outside.

This realization then becomes the freedom of not needing to attach to things that are temporal for your eternal value. If we don't come to this realization, we will never have the revelation that we were created for more. We will just be living in search of meaning. A job, a better car, slimmer, fatter, more this, and more that. YOU were created for way more than that. The fleetingness of their satisfaction is merely a veil to the real you. The real meaning and purpose for your life is to sow seeds that will build the next generation and beyond. You are unique with a unique story and with that, you can be a world changer.

How Do You Find the Core You?

When we are devoid of time or form we can move forward in the process of our Being (Core), which brings us closer to enlightenment and God. Subject and object become harmoniously intertwined. When Jesus said the "Truth will set you free," this meant once we free ourselves of form or body, we can step into the realm of Being. A spirit Being that is eternal, thus freeing us from fear of temporality or vulnerability. You can then leave the life as a caterpillar behind and step into your full destiny as a butterfly. You no longer need to live a limited life in captivity to worldly false paradigms and statistics. Your life can be without walls or bounds.

The body as you see it is just a container for the real you. The visible part of the body is a false perception of the real you. The real you cannot be defined by what you see. The true definition is in what you cannot see. It is from an ability to see from inside/out that the true Being can be connected. If we look at our lives as just our birth and death, we are living an illusion. A mind-boxed facade of what you really are. An artificial, deceptive veil to reality.

Beneath your container (body), are mind, spirit, and soul. A magnificent miracle that began as a microscopic seed. If this is not miraculous enough, wait for it … fearfully and wonderfully made, in the likeness of God. Because it is so beyond our grasp it is fearfully and wonderfully made. This is beyond our human ability to rationalize, study, or even come close to comprehending. It takes us out of our limitations of space and time, and into a deeper meaning, of timeless infinity.

Question: "What does it mean that we are fearfully and wonderfully made? (Psalm 139:14)"

Answer: Psalm 139:14 declares, "I praise you because I am fearfully and wonderfully made; your works are wonderful,

I know that full well." The context of this verse is the incredible nature of our physical bodies. The human body is the most complex and unique organism in the world, and that complexity and uniqueness speaks volumes about the mind of its Creator. Every aspect of the body, down to the tiniest microscopic cell, reveals that it is fearfully and wonderfully made." (Cited thc-ministry)

As long as your mind is influenced by what you see, you cannot connect to the greater part of you. It's in retraining the mind from "seeing to believe it," to just believing it. The greater is always in the unseen moving the seen. The unseen then becomes seen as we go through life becoming a testimony of its goodness by what we have now overcome. There is Glory in your story, as you are now standing in what you have overcome to get to this moment.

We have been conditioned by society and its patterns to live in a life of limitations by conforming to its paradigms. This is a misperception of our reality, as we are not our body, but an eternal spirit Being experiencing a human moment. This false belief is spurred by fear, and our birth in separation to God (carnal). When this separation is bridged, we begin to live the life that He intended for us. Our carnal existence, which is founded in the flesh, further eludes our mind from our real self.

Adding appendages to find what is missing will keep your life in bondage, as you will seek it in relationships, the opinion of others, career, education, and money. When this doesn't satisfy, which believe me, after 20 years of doing this it will certainly not, you will start to do everything too much. Date too much. Work too much. Study too much. Stress too much. The result will be hitting a Prozac wall in the hope of finding escape and refuge from the exhaustion off all the too muches. It becomes a tiresome, lonely hunt to find that it brings nothing at all.

The agent (conduit) to making a connection to your true self will never be in adding something outside of yourself, as nothing from the outside can feed the inside. The Truth can only be found from within. The internal revelation of an external manifestation. The inner self is the bridge to Being. Pure connectedness to Oneness, eternal and forever living in your true self, which is in the likeness of God (The Creator). Instinctively we have known this all along. The stories we read in fairy tales reveal a magical connection between narratives of disguise and a metamorphosis to something permanent and authentic. In the story of "Beauty and the Beast," the beast must win the beautiful girl's heart in order to be transformed back into the prince he once was; The Ugly Duckling turned into the swan he always was. Fairy tales stimulate a different dimension of our minds, to the contemplation of being just a transporter to a yet unseen reality that we are not Master over. In the same way, we have known who we are all along and just needed a conduit to reunite with a core self. Our conduit is in getting a touch from our maker, God.

Moving Away from Living by Our Five Senses

Once you get a hold of this, you will no longer depend or be affected by what is on the outside. This increased state of awareness of the spirit within will be a catalyst for rapid life change and transformation. You will no longer be bound to an illusion to the things of this world and its patterns. As you increase in this state of awareness, your light will gather strength. In the same way a forest fire can be started with a strike of a match, this metamorphosis of self will gather momentum and power. The more you meditate and dwell in this state, the greater your connection to your true self. You will no longer be centered in your mind, or the external world. You will be at oneness with God. You will still have thoughts and emotions, but they will no longer be the master of you, as the God on the inside of you will be far greater.

Quieting the Mind to Hear God

It is through having greater presence, stillness, and sense of Being that you are able to connect deeper with God. With all our daily functions and tasks, on top of approximately 60,000 thoughts per day, we need to really quiet things down. Take note of where your mind is now. Are you focused on this text, or are you thinking of tasks that you need to do later today? That is the focus of your attention. There may also be some mind chatter. This could be in the form of your mind-box editing what you are hearing or what you are reading. Try not to let this drown out and compete for your attention. By quelling this thought pattern, you can then hear the voice of God. Begin to practice hearing the voice from within, so that you are not hearing the noise and clutter from outside.

Do not let the external world be your only focus. Connect to your inner self. The world will still be present, but you will be seeing it from the inside out. As you develop and nurture this state of inner awareness, you will find greater connectedness and presence. Your focus will be like you have not experienced previously. There will be a calm stillness about you. Your true inner self will be connected to God in a deeper way at all times. You can go deeper, as He will no longer be competing with all the noise. You can practice this while driving in traffic jams, standing in long lines at coffee shops and airports, or any other opportunity when you would usually be in your head. This will aid you to new levels and a whole new way of living. During this process in the coming weeks, take note of how this has improved your attention and state of Being. When grounded in mind and spirit, and both are deeply connected, nothing can shake you anymore. Your spirit mind will be grounded in the unmovable, unchangeable, unshakable God. Remember, your ability to hear from God is only as good as your ability to focus your mind.

Unless you develop a state of presence and stillness, the mind, through conditioning, societal patterns, and the limitations within those paradigms, will always be competing for God's attention. In the old mold, there will be times of stillness, but as we are reacting off everything around us, we are at its mercy. This is our human state and the innate mind of captivity. When a person sounds his or her car horn, hears negative media, or reacts based on interactions with others during his or her daily life, he or she then goes into the limbic mind. This can be compared to a plane on autopilot, as when our mind goes into this predetermined pattern, it reacts to the things from around. This is a script that many of us spend our entire lives hostage to.

To make a change, there must first be an awareness of these patterns. Then a breaking down to bring in the new. Notice how you react to media news, others' driving, environments, and all the things around you. You will be surprised how little stimulus it takes for your emotional, scripted mind to take over. In this state, your spirit mind is diminished by your carnal mind. In effect you are controlled by your mind. To break this pattern, notice when you go into your mind. Then notice the triggers. Is it in traffic? While listening to news media? During perceived loss? When you are losing? Reacting to what people say? During quiet time? When you get up in the morning? All these are external variables that you are reacting to intrinsically. You are not able to see the world how it is, but instead you see it how you are. The more you enter stillness and Being, the more you will find yourself reacting independently of the variables all around you. Compare a torch to a halogen lamp; the halogen lamp is infinitely brighter. It is not changed by smoke or fog, as it continues to shine through all conditions when they arise. When your strength is based on your spirit (inside), the mind of patterns and fear is brought down. The old paradigm is shifted, giving way to a mind of faith and inner peace.

In the Bible, which I refer to as the "human operant handbook," Jeremiah wrote "They will be like a tree planted by the water that sends out its roots by the stream. It does not fear when heat comes; its leaves are always green. It has no worries in a year of drought and never fails to bear fruit." (Cited biblegateway.com). How this can translate in our lives is that as long as our inner core is planted on an invariable in a variable world, we are no longer at the mercy of our circumstances when things change. We have a state of deep Being and a deeper connection to God. This has been born from new levels of stillness and calmness in us. We are now able to be the change in our circumstance, not the circumstance the change in us. We are no longer living in our mind, which is fear-based; we are living by the spirit within greater connection to God.

When you reclaim the mind you were first created with, you will get into alignment with all your life was meant to be. This is the life before your mind was conditioned through negative words spoken over you, your experiences, then taking on societal patterns and norms. When you practice stillness and focus, you will step into consciousness and be more connected to the inner you, your true Being. The more you do this, the less you will be in your script of who you think you are, or for that matter think that you need to be. You will be walking in your divine purpose that you were uniquely created for. The days of taking and competing will be over. You will no longer be in the "rat race," "dog eat dog" of this world. Instead, you will be a giver and not a taker. Purpose-filled and not in need of finding, as you would have found what you had all along, before the mind veiled Truth for you to think otherwise. When in this state of consciousness, you are living in the likeness of God and have no concept of the confines of the mind. God knows the beginning, middle, and end of all things as consciousness is in all creation and has no limits or separation that govern boundaries of time or space. It's a constant, uninterrupted line of timelessness.

This changed my life from challenge to opportunity, regrets to all things working for my good, sadness to joy, weariness to renewed vigor, staleness of routine to an opportunity to step out and do something new. I no longer need to add or find, as my value is from within, so I no longer remain without.

Sounds Great but How Can I Get My Head around It?

Let's break it down:

Sensory living: In separation, ego based, subject to fear, influenced by changing circumstances, duality, detached from the source, constricted by time.

Living by natural law: In control, using reason, analytical, inventive, relies on virtues by human research, explores the reaches of time.

Conscious living: Fully creative, full of potential, not confined to time limitations, in tune with Being, grounded in source. Knowing God in a relational way.

Exercise:

This is one for your mind. How do I understand how close I stand to my source?

Take the passenger of a roller coaster. They have no idea of design, are fearful if they haven't tried it before, their mind is painting a picture of how it might be, start to wonder what may happen.

Take the member of staff working on it. They have knowledge about the basic operation, are not fearful because they know the ride, may think that it has danger, but not focused on that aspect so much.

Take the manufacturer. They designed it, are not fearful, as they know the start and end of the journey, and have a deep belief and conviction in what they do.

To help you understand the progression of scale in proximity to source.

The passenger: This represents the carnal person living a life of separation to source. They want what they can get out of it for themselves, but are often affected by changing circumstances.

Fearful.

The member of staff: This represents a person with an awareness of a higher power, living a life that they are trying to work to their advantage. This may involve going to a higher power for the things that they want, or when a challenge comes their way. Mostly living a life as a free spirit.

The manufacturer: This represents a person living a life knowing God in a relational way, all things coming through Him, and a surrendering control and letting Him take over. They are grounded in faith and do not fear. They are no longer striving but are thriving in life.

CHAPTER NINE

Why We Hold Back

A lot of the things we do today are based upon events experienced in our pasts. These things keep us in our comfort zone. This is a place where things are comfortable and familiar, so we tend to stay there because we fear that new actions may not work out for us so we'd rather not chance it. Thus, we don't step out of our box and make a change.

There are many reasons we hold ourselves back. For example, if we want a new job, we may go into the interview and think, "They're never going to hire me. I'm not good enough for this job." Perhaps this attitude stems from parents who told us, "You can't do anything well; you are not good enough at the things you do," or "You will never amount to anything." This would hamper the development of our self-esteem and cause us to have self-doubt as a way of protecting ourselves from being hurt or disappointed.

How do we know we can't do something unless we are judging it based on our past experiences? The only thing we can judge accurately is the very moment we're living. Anything we judge about what may happen in the future, even if it's only a day from now, is based upon supposition and our own self-contained reality. One of my favorite sayings is: "It's not a tragedy that we all die, but that it takes so many of us so long to live." We put our minds on a leash and stop ourselves from being open to the opportunities that come our way. Stress is interest paid on something that may not happen tomorrow.

Another way we hold ourselves back is by saying that we are getting old. This is our way of affirming that we will not be good at certain things, which develops a habit of avoiding things that we might still be able to do well but will never know about since we won't try them. There are some things that we will certainly not be as good at as we age, yet many people still run marathons well into their 80s and 90s. Remember that the world is as we see it, not as it really is.

Today, if you remove your mind chatter from it, is just today. All days are created equally, and all days are great. People say "It's a great day because it's Friday." What they are really saying is that it's a great day because they do not have to work the next day, which means that their life was on hold until this day came. Plenty of us live our lives with a form of "destination sickness," where we focus on getting to some particular date on the calendar. What ends up happening is that all the days in between now and then end up becoming a forgotten blur, as the focus only rests on one place. It is the days in between that make up the bulk of our time on earth, and it's a shame to squander the blessings that are revealed in our everyday lives because our focus is on tomorrow.

Push pause for a second and think back to when you were a child sitting beside a swimming pool, afraid that the water was too deep. That fear was based in what you could not clearly see. That's not unlike many of the fears you have today. The fact that you can't see the outcome is what's holding you back. It's easy to stay in this place, not really going anywhere, just residing in the self-imposed mind jail and its comfort zone.

Thoughts of an unknown outcome or the fear of other people's reactions are what typically hold us back, not the things, opportunities or people themselves. By raising our consciousness and seeing our thoughts as just thoughts and not foregone conclusions, we can unravel the things that are holding us back. When we practice stepping out of our editing and mind chatter, we can bridge the gap between our defeatist thoughts and the great opportunities that are in front of us. We can be victors and not victims.

Fears creep up from time to time, but that doesn't mean we need to live by them. We can instead transform and renew our minds. It's not an easy or fast thing to do, as we can only overcome our fears slowly and with much practice and patience. As with any change, it is best to make progress that is consistent rather than erratic, as only the former makes for lasting changes.

To move forward, allow yourself to experience uncomfortable moments, as this will help you identify the things that hold you back. Remember that in order to change, we must do something different and that often causes discomfort, but with repetition, uncomfortable emotions will start to feel comfortable, much like staying in our comfort zone feels today. A temporary inconvenience is required to make a change, which is not nearly as inconvenient as living in fear and missing out on life.

It's easier to stay on one side of the street than it is to cross the street, as crossing the street takes effort. Imagine if we never exerted effort in the context of our lives—we'd be standing still and living with only a fraction of our purpose. If we do not raise our awareness, we may spend all of our time walking in an ever-faster circle with the assumption that we are making progress. It is better to walk in a slow, straight line than a faster and faster circle. If we let fear stand between us and our dreams, whether subconsciously or knowingly, we can eventually abandon them altogether and live life by justifying our circumstances.

What will help get us out of this learned pattern of living is to realize that we have chosen this way of life and have a choice to begin a refresh, starting as quickly as today. We can transform our thoughts by changing our perspective and turn our fears into the drive and energy we need to achieve positive results. By moving our perspective away from the difficulty of doing something to what needs to be done to achieve the goal, we change our focus from what's difficult to what's possible. This builds confidence and leads to taking action instead of more reasons to not do something. Fear will be replaced with courage. Possibility is what we put our focus on, as whatever we focus on expands, while fear only brings more fear. Thoughts create actions, and those actions create our life.

As with most things that are significant, writing them down on a vision board or sheet of paper can help clarify them. Write down what your fears might be and then include an action plan on how to overcome them. Identify what the outcome may be when each fear is overturned. Similarly, focus on what the benefits are of overcoming each fear, with the knowledge that the benefits outweigh the risks of maintaining the fear. With time, fears will become less significant as you can learn how to easily move past them. Then a new world of endless possibility will open up.

Remember that fear is a choice, and we can just as easily make a choice to not allow fear to deny us the life we want. Fear is faith but faith in the wrong thing. Don't wait for circumstances to change before you do something, as this will never happen. The right time is always now, and the change can always be made from within. We only have this one life, so why hold back? Why not give it your all? Why not be the change to your circumstance?

Defeating Giants in Your Life

Do you ever feel like you are walking up a mountain, a slippery slope that at the time appears to have no end? Do you feel like it's one thing after another, a constant battle? It can very often be the same things that come up: sin, anger, or depression. This is because until we really face them face-to-face, they are a cyclical pattern that continues to rear its ugly head with vengeance.

As humans I am certain that we can all relate. We all, from time to time, come up against the same challenges of temptations, weariness, frustration, anger, and insecurities. In whatever area the struggle, we have found ourselves wandering in the wilderness, looking for answers with no apparent solution. Whatever we do or wherever we go, we feel like David with Goliath staring us down! What are we doing in our quest to overcome this giant? Are we building our own muscles and relying on our own strength, or relying on the One who has overcome the world? It's important to know who we enter the battle with, our own might, which is emotional and has a propensity to magnify the situation or circumstance, or the Advocate who can administer calm, insight, and resolution to the battle. We all know the story of Pharaoh's army. They were mighty, but within one miraculous moment plunged to their death in the Red Sea.

The fact is that we all have a choice of who we battle our giants with. Our own might or the might of the One who never tires or fails?

Goliath was David's giant and also Israel's to overcome. Even though the spirit of God had departed from Saul, he was still leading the army of Israelites in battle against the Philistines. Saul and his men would wake up day after day facing their giant. This was the problem. They looked at their problem and not the solution. The Philistines sent out Goliath to distract Saul and his army. Their ploy worked, as it kept Saul and his army confused and disheartened. The Philistines chose Goliath, while the Israelites chose to hide and run.

Into the scene walks a little shepherd boy called David. He is all by himself with nothing much more than a packed lunch that he was picking up for himself and his three elder brothers. When he arrives at the camp he can hear Goliath's voice ridiculing the Israelites and their God. He couldn't understand why men gathered as an entire army would bow down to just one man. So David asked Saul (1 Samuel 17:29) "Is there not a cause?"

David was used by God to conquer Goliath. This was no normal man, as he stood 9 feet, 9 inches and wore armor. He was aware of the challenge but instead put his focus on the solution. He could easily have remained fearful and focused on the giant with the scary, armored appearance. After all it worked in scaring an entire Israelite army, stopping them in their tracks. Goliath stood in the valley for 40 days shouting at the Israelites to fight him. Goliath wanted God's people to give up on Him and instead serve his people. There is some significance in the numbers associated with Goliath, his height, 6 cubits, 6 pieces of armor, and a spear weighing 600 shekels. The threefold repetition of the number 6; 666 is a reference to the enemy Satan (Revelation 13:18). David was aware of the challenge he was facing, and knew he could not lean on his own understanding. Nevertheless, he was determined to confront what stood in front of him and defeat it. He defeated the giant because he had the right heart and conviction. He kept his eyes on His God who is way bigger than any circumstance or giant.

What Does This Mean to Me?

Goliath was directing his attack on the people of Israel. They were the chosen people of God, and David had been anointed and appointed to lead them. What this means to you is that at times giants are going to rear up against you. David knew that Goliath would not back down and that he would need to be confronted and defeated. Life can present us with many emotional hurts and disappointments. What giant are you facing in your life? 1) This could be a failed marriage that has left you with guilt that you don't seem able to shake, 2) abuse that has left you feeling shamed and hurt, 3) financial problems, 4) anger toward another, 5) addictive behavior, 6) loneliness, 7) health issues, or 8) depression.

Whichever area you can relate to, if it's not confronted head on, it can become a giant in your life. If it remains without being overcome, it can keep you stuck for many years, and maybe the rest of your life. When we look at the giant in front of us, our vision becomes obscured as we see the obstacle more than the solution. If we allow the obstacle or giant to be bigger than what we use to overcome it, how can we defeat it? If we change perspective we can change the way we see our giants. God allows them to make you stronger and prepare you to defeat the bigger ones yet to come. So look at giants as an opportunity to defeat and conquer. As you read this, the very moment you are now in is a tribute to all that you have been through and overcome to get here. I suggest that you sit down in a quiet place, to slow your mind so that you can develop a clear mental picture of the giants that you want to conquer in your life. Then write them down in order of their significance, the most significant to least significant. This will help you to realize that they are not really your biggest battle, as it is the mind that has made them your giants. Although these may appear very real to you, remember that this has only been manifest in your life as they have become your main focus. When you put your main focus on God, you will begin to see them in a different light. You will begin to see them as mountains you can either climb or remove from your life. By changing our focus from our problem to the God in the problem, we get hope, renewal, and the possibilities of what is coming out from the giants or circumstances. we presently face. This turns the giant into our opportunity and not our foe. Very simply, our present focus determines our future destination.

Every triumph is a result of a challenge. Every miracle did not begin without a problem being there first. Jesus fed 5,000 with five loaves and two fish. Why? Because they were hungry. He healed a lady who had been bleeding for 12 years. Why? Because she was lame. He gave sight to the blind. Why? Because they could not see. If we are to ever be victors in our circumstances (giants), we must first change our perspective of the situation.

I can personally tell out of the greatest afflictions in my life that I have gained the greatest enlightenment. Overcoming addictive behaviors. My father's funeral wake on my mother's birthday in 2008. My mother dying in my arms in a hospital bed from complications of a tragic accident as soon as I landed after an 11 hour-plane journey. Mother's

Day the day after I preached at her funeral two weeks later. I have used all of these giants to gain strength, wisdom, and gratitude. I am a victor and not a victim. There is Glory in my story. I give God all the Glory. Without Him I would have been dead in my prideful human nature. Please don't let pride come between you and the greatest life possible. You don't have to live life as a victim of your circumstances, as you can live as a victor in them. The battle is never the circumstance, as the real battle is with your mind. When David defeated Goliath, others were encouraged. You are being observed by your colleagues, friends, and family. When you are faced with a challenge, it's the way that you handle that challenge that will become your testimony to God. Do not look at the challenge. Instead, look at God in your challenge. Whatever you are facing, you can overcome and have a greater life than you could ever dream, comprehend, or imagine.

CHAPTER TEN

Letting Loose

This is an area a lot of us struggle with, as people around us as well as the media put the focus on negative news instead of positive events. This creates a very uptight, stressed-out bunch of people living in this modern world. We are surrounded by this negativity from an early age, and by the time we reach adulthood, we readily become drawn to all the tragic events in the world.

Changing perspective makes all the difference, as the way we see the world directly affects the way we live. In order to live a more free-flowing, loose lifestyle, we need to place our focus beyond ourselves and look at the big picture. When our predominant focus is on self, a self-obsessed existence results and gives us a slant on life that is very narrow. This makes it challenging for us to have a lighter way of moving through things. We all have goals and responsibilities that, if not balanced, can push us into a life of discomfort and stress. Unless we recognize and take steps to repair the stress, our joy will be hampered, and we may move through life with a very serious outlook, missing the greatness that becomes revealed in the small of our daily routine.

Things can seem like a big deal to us from the smallness of our individual existence, with each new thing compounding upon itself until everything is blown out of proportion. We then go into the what-if, uptight mode of living. We need to look beyond our noses and adopt a bigger outlook, so we begin to revolve with the world as opposed to the world revolving around us.

Our modern world is very self-focused and unhappy, full of self-obsessed, uptight people on a miserable path of their own making. To embark on a smoother, more flowing life, it's good to sit back and observe the people around us, as this helps us gain a deeper awareness of our own behavior. People generally adapt to the energy around them, unless they develop a greater consciousness and make a consistent effort to renew their minds with change.

What helped me find awareness was coming to the realization that I am only a speck in the eons of time, and that in the thousands of years before and after my time on earth, my life is only a vapor that will vanish before I know it. With this in mind, why would I worry about things out of my control? Instead, I decided to make every moment count. After all, worry and stress are like paying interest on something that may not ever happen. This realization made me less serious and helped me take my focus off myself and instead put it onto the world and people, making my life freer, more flowing and joyous. This translated to being excited about life and living in the realm where all things work together for the greater good.

We spend so much of our lives putting off a great deal of things that we want to do because our mind chatter makes us think that we have more pressing issues and circumstances to deal with. In truth, our minds have created this as being our reality, which will never change until we change from within, so that our outlook will appear different and impact our choices positively.

Steps for Adjusting Outlook

Ask yourself what you would do today if you were not so serious. Think of how you would invest your time if you knew that this day was to be your last. Write down all the things that you would do and include the time you need for those things to happen. By doing this, your mind will start to focus on those things and see them as being possible. Your attitude will change to one that's lighter and more flexible. When we get over ourselves, we can live a life that is more open to doing a variety of different things that we didn't think were possible before. Also, by taking the focus off of ourselves, pressures fall right off, leaving us to move forward and be the person we were destined to be. When we let go, possibility takes over, and very soon we will not recognize our new life.

The challenges and tests we face are not unique to us, yet we can develop an acceptance of them by letting go of emotional baggage. This will help us look forward to each day, seeing it as a brand-new opportunity to live our lives to the fullest.

Circumstances are hard to change; however, we can change outcomes by changing ourselves within our circumstances.

For example, while we are driving, our mind chatter may say, "There will be no parking when we get to the store." Yet when we get there, we find a parking spot right outside, but rather than being happy about that, we move onto the next complaint: "The store is going to be packed full of people." Yet when we go inside, it's quiet and there are only a few people there.

This is just one example of how we make assumptions that are not based on reality that create a big negative impact on our quality of life. They are based on the false interpretations of our life experiences. This has nothing to do with what actually exists. Our interpretations involve accumulated disappointments experienced over many years, which demolish the potential of the present moment through our mind jail of the past.

Imagine a beautiful, sunny day when you're looking through a clean window that is sprayed with furniture polish, causing it to turn muddy and smeared. Running a finger through the polish only adds to the smudges, making that sunny day suddenly very gray. Mind jails make us see our whole lives through smudges. These things become habitual; we don't just smudge occasionally. We add that polish all the time and reduce the potential of each day. The only way to change that is by changing our mind-set to seeing the clean window and beautiful day without the polish that our mind has created. Because the day is abundant and unlimited, so we should see it accurately.

To begin the process of letting loose, have an inner dialog with yourself anytime you feel a negative thought coming in. Examine why that thought is present, and go to a place of redirection by resolution. This will help improve every area of your life, as letting loose can become apparent first through identifying patterns in thinking. Once we know those patterns and rationalize why they exist, we can overcome them and get into a habit of no longer thinking through them. After all, the way we think today happened as a result of a habit we've developed over years.

Many of us spend a lot of money on feel-good books, seminars, and courses in an attempt to snap out of feeling blue only to find their effects fleeting. Because, after a while, something superficial and negligible will come in to push our buttons, sending us back into that familiar spiral of negative thinking. Then we wonder why such everyday, trivial events smack us in the face time and time again. The answer is that the source of our unhappiness has never been addressed; it's merely been covered up for a short while. No matter how many self-help magazines we read or seminars we attend, painting over the rot only gives us a superficially positive exterior. Deep down, our hearts will not reflect our shiny appearance.

But if we examine why we're thinking that way, we can re-program ourselves into a habit of thinking positively. The only way we can change a habit is by learning a newer, and in this case better, habit. The essential component in this is to become aware that our thoughts reflect the way we feel and that we all have the capability to control them.

To override your thoughts, practice replacing each negative thought with a positive one. As with anything in life, whatever we focus on expands. Also be mindful of the people you surround yourself with. As the old sayings go, "Birds of a feather flock together" and "Misery loves company." A person often becomes like the people they spend time with. It's important to remember that other people's mind-sets do not have to impact yours and that you are a separate entity who can decide how you will feel rather than somebody else making the decision for you. After all, nobody makes us feel a certain way. That is entirely our choice.

To make a change, write down positive thoughts and affirmations after negative thoughts and affirmations. Place them on a vision board in your home or office so you can be reminded to think positively throughout the course of your day.

This could look something like: (Negative response/Positive response) "Why did this person cut me off while driving?" / "There is plenty of space for both of us. They may just be having a bad day." "The line at the store will be long." / "The line at the store will move quickly and efficiently." "Why aren't they answering their telephone? Don't they want to talk to me?" / "They are doing a good job and are probably in demand. I'll call back later."

Remember that our words form our thoughts and our thoughts create our reality. Never underestimate the significance of a word, because it is very powerful. It can transform one moment into a reality that can impact the rest of our lives. Every thought is also significant, as it is the predicator of how we act. We flow where the mind goes, as the two are integral. Let us program our minds for the life that we want and not let the mind give us the life that we follow.

Resisting Change

The biggest obstacle we have as human beings to making a change is our resistance to it. Resistance creates a barrier between us and the changes we want in our lives, be they in our habits, job, relationships, or any other area that may require doing something we are not accustomed to. Resistance can come from many places, such as a fear of failure, feelings of losing control, or various deep-seeded insecurities.

Resisting change is often developed in childhood when we are not given a choice about whether we want to do certain things, which force us to conform to the demands placed on us. This predicates a feeling that change is akin to losing control over our lives. In adulthood, this can manifest as reinforcing control by resisting change, which leads to rigidity in people. Even in simple things, when we are asked to change our nutrition, medications, or personal habits, this can trigger our stubborn, learned resistance.

There are many things in life that force us to make changes, such as circumstantial events thrown upon us without our choosing, be it losing a job, a divorce, a downturn in our health, or the death of a loved one. All these things make us feel uncomfortable, because the instability of events we cannot control makes us uncertain of our future.

Essentially, our ego tells us, "I don't want to change because

I want to stay in control." The ego is an integral part of living, yet the key is to keep the ego in check by not attaching our self-worth to eternal desires, accolades, and possessions. The ego can never feel whole, as it's born from a separation between the universe and us. In this way, it creates a state of disconnection with life. By keeping the ego to a minimum, however, we can flow with the universe and not be as attached to things and circumstances. When we can see past our ego, we are no longer influenced by its force and will find ourselves letting go of it. With this in mind, every time we feel a reaction within us based on an external circumstance, we can dilute the experience by examining the source of our feelings.

It helps to identify the areas in our lives where we have the greatest resistance and then understand the source of this resistance, as it's never based on the event in front of us. Most of us fear change, not because we fear letting something different into our lives, but because we fear that we will be doing something wrong, or that we will not live up to other people's expectations of us. We may also resist change when we are obligated to do something. At that time, we feel that we are submitting control over our lives to somebody else who is forcing a change upon us. This can be something as mundane as a traffic attendant telling us to move our vehicle, or being asked to fill out a form at the Department of Motor Vehicles.

Side Effects of Resisting Change:

Ill feelings toward others: This can be revealed by engaging in gossip, complaining about people, and feeling consumed by other people's lives and beliefs.

Oversleeping: This can be evident in overuse of the snooze button, or in a general lack of zest when getting out of bed in the morning.

Drama: This results in a struggle with the people and circumstances in our daily lives. We may begin to find comfort in the chaos so that we continue to stay in turmoil, as this becomes the food that nourishes this cycle.

Blaming others: This manifests in looking to other people instead of ourselves to assume responsibility for our situations in life.

Bad habits: These can include spending too much while shopping, drinking too much, or eating compulsively.

This way of living is exhausting and usually leaves us looking at other people or outside circumstances as the causes of our unhappy situations, when they are, in fact, perpetuated by our attitude to the external circumstances we are resisting. This can create a vicious cycle, as we look to external changes for internal changes. This will never work, as we must instead come to an awareness and acceptance that we are responsible for our own lives and that any fix we try to make will be short-lived until we fix what the real problem is.

Ways to Overcome Resistance:

Put your faith and focus in something bigger than yourself, whether it's religious beliefs or a longstanding goal you want to accomplish.

Examine your heart and get in touch with what you want to do in your life by becoming aware of how you feel in certain circumstances. Write down your feelings and use them as a reference when dealing with situations as they arise. This will assist you in having an inner dialog with yourself when external circumstances begin to affect how you feel about yourself.

Put your focus on the benefits that change can bring and take your mind off the challenges to reduce the influence that negativity has on you, which will reduce your resistance to change.

All changes are ultimately for our benefit if we perceive them to be. Seeing all changes, even the painful ones, as positive will open us up to embracing them as they are a constant in life. If we want to change our lives, be it a habit or choice we consistently keep making, changing the way we think will be the catalyst that allows us to see the change through. It is only by doing what we are not good at doing at the present moment that we can undo the things that are holding us back. By contrast, staying the same as we are today may be comfortable in the short term, but this approach will dramatically limit our lives. Remember: When we change the way we see things, the things we see change.

If our resistance is fear-based, it has probably stemmed from a long-held fear, usually one that started in childhood. If our resistance is control-based, it can also come from childhood, but is more focused on our fear of losing control over our lives and being at the mercy of other people or institutions. We may feel as though we are not allowed to make decisions for ourselves anymore. In both cases, we need to establish where the issue originated if we really intend to overcome it.

Establishing the source and coming to terms with our past so we may rise above it helps to gradually open us up to making changes. It's not going to happen overnight and can't be flipped like a switch on a radio. We need to work on ourselves first by constantly being aware of our feelings and their sources and then move forward gradually until we're comfortable with change and no longer associate it with something negative. Like any long-term solution, it can only be achieved one step at a time, one decision at a time and one day at a time.

Take, for example, the act of filling out documents. In place of our usual response to put up resistance, we can stay open-minded and see our actions as complying with a system that's going to work for us rather than against us. We can re-contextualize the process as one where we don't actually lose control but gain advancement and benefits. Through it all, we can reinforce a more positive mind-set by telling ourselves, "I'm not going to get abandoned. I'm valuable and this is necessary. I'm going to be OK and trust life to take care of me in the way it always has in the past."

When we react to a task negatively, it is our unconscious mind that distorts our perception of the task to maintain the systematic way we have always dealt with things in our lives. In this way, our behavior acts like an addiction, so it's maintained. This gives us the green light to continue the behavior. Only by developing a "feel-good recall" can we begin to associate good feelings with new behaviors and actions, which will perpetuate them and make lasting positive changes. Of course, the hardest part of this is the first step, though harder still would be living a life with bad habits we never tried hard enough to break.

CHAPTER ELEVEN

Living a Life Beyond Walls

We have traveled through this book together, and we are now beginning a new journey. It's a new day for your destiny, your relationships, your thoughts and dreams. Everything is going to be different. Let's use this moment to be the most significant in our lives, by taking ownership of our thoughts and actions today. We now have the tools to have an entirely new way of living to a higher level by our new way of thinking. To have the fullest life, we need to be living it and not just thinking why it's not different. We have started a fire by lighting an inner spark that will soon burn as a forest fire. Let's now live to a new level of richness and well-being.

If we view our body as a mosaic of living cells, we can take a hold of the reality that all things are working together for our good. Each of these cells is created to assist the others to work to a higher level, even dying off to give birth to others. This creates a shift, a radical change: one order is dying and another coming. This paradigm is in existence to advance all things in our human corporeal organism. We are the interface of connectedness to all that is present by our thoughts and actions, which are working as a collective ripple in the vastness of the Milky Way and Universe beyond. All things are now working together for your good. You no longer live a life in duality with the world around you, but find yourself in unity that rewards you with inner peace, joyousness, and contentment.

You are probably thinking "What has this got to do with me?" Everything! You are mind, body, and soul. An intertwining masterpiece made up of a myriad of parts that flow from the estuary of the heart that impact the spirit Being of you as a person. This is then manifest as a fine ballet of the bodily system of the mental, spirit life of man. A trinity that meshes all things to come together. When we balance all these functioning parts, we harmonize and fine-tune ourselves to be no longer a fragmented and weakened product of our life's experiences. Instead we empower ourselves to be functioning in Being to go on and lead the life that was Divinely intended for each one of us. We are no longer a product of our circumstances, as we now stand as a victor in what we have come through.

In our childhoods, we were taught the game of "I." We have been well prepared to go on a lonely road called ego. This has led to a life of striving for personal achievement and conquests, and one that too often brings us to feeling alone and isolated. Our modern day connectivity has reared up as a serpent against us and become our pain of disconnectedness. In the same way as the caterpillar transformed into a butterfly, you have now transformed into your true-self (Being). You have moved to a new level of living not dictated and molded to fit into cultural norms. You are free, as you are no longer in bondage to the pursuit of pleasure and storing for the self. You are aware that following the ego is a choice and not the only way of life available to you. Gone are the days of competing and fighting for the things that you need, as there is an inner calm as you are now connected to your own individual story. As you are no longer driven by competing, you are on a course to build your family, your friends, and the world all around you. You are not now living in fear because someone may get something before you, as you know you have what you need to complete your individual journey.

In this bodily metamorphosis, you are no longer living in a separated state due to the overwhelming drive of the ego, which can only cause the breaking down of purpose as it survives only through the striving of getting, competing, to then breaking down, to eventually imploding. You are built up from the inside out. There is a calmness that permeates your entire body from within a changed estuary that flows from the depths of your heart. While acknowledging the reality that ego will always be a part of us, we will not compete with it in a futile attempt to thwart it, but instead let the newness in you be driven by Divine intention and not human separation. As the caterpillar becoming a butterfly is a product of change from one form becoming another, your new life will be from one thing changing to another. In our case, a change occurs by how we now see things on the inside that would have predicated the changes on the outside. With the ego and desire integral but kept in balance, they are no longer dueling for your purpose, but now used as the coals that sustain the new level of living you will now experience.

The world is in you; however, you are not veiled by it, as you have realized that you are to be the change in it. It's out of this growing awareness that will predicate the constant renewal of the mind because of your new focus. You are no longer conforming to the worldly paradigms and the patterns that can only result in separation from Being and true purpose. You are now in your true purpose with a new focus that will ultimately determine a new destination for your life. Your corporeal journey may contain countless steps; your spiritual journey only has one: the step you are taking right now. As your awareness grows, you realize that the step you're in now is a container to all the others, and then within those, your destination. Ultimately within this type of posture, the comprehension of God being in all of them from the beginning, middle, and end.

Your personal and work relationships will explode to new levels of joyousness, success, and satisfaction. Through the intertwining of body, mind, and spirit, a greater sense of awareness will coalesce within the depths of your heart that will bring about new levels of empathy and love toward all others around you. It is within this mood of balance that judgment will be made acceptance, argument made discussion, taking from made adding to, resentment made forgiveness, and with it a life full of internal satisfaction and joyousness. As your mind will have less mind chatter and negative self- talk, you will find a new grace in your communicative skills. You will no longer be making a movie in your mind with all the noise and chatter previously present. Your attention will be more focused as you have quieted down all the internal negative influences. During interactions with others, you will no longer be governed by the things that they once triggered within you, as you will be experiencing forgiveness and freedom from past pain and hurts. You will be more aware of others reacting off one another, but you will not get ensnared, instead making a choice to communicate more freely and effectively.

The world outside will no longer be the place that you will seek for your answers, as you will be connected to your

Divine plan and purpose for your life. In this increased state of Being, you will be driven by the spirit, and in so, renewed and fulfilled to perpetuate a state of purpose. You will be full of potential, as you will realize that things are not given to you at their potential, but are given full of potential. As you are in a state of oneness between creator and purpose, you be full of life and not drained by stress or fear.

In this new state of connectedness, there will be an inertia about you that will sustain itself regardless of what is going on on the outside. As your inner self will now impact all that is around you, there will no longer be a need to escape the false reality (your interpretation) and lose yourself in "too much" behaviors. Your independence from worldly influences will translate to you being the master of your destiny, as you will no longer be driven by a need to get, beat, or compete, as you will be founded in God and His plan and purpose, which are just for you. There will be no inner struggle and resistance to either trying to change others or circumstances, as what you focus on will now be a mirror that will become that change.

Within this new perspective will be a greater zest within you, as life will have attained a certain flow that will be sustained in times of test as well as triumph. Your days will be akin to waves splashing on a shoreline. One experience will set you up for another, and interactions will now be a place to impart, learn, and grow. The mystery of your journey will have no horizon, as the freedom of your inner self will be guided through revelation in your experiences. One thing is certain: the ebbs and flows of life will be forever shifting, but you will not be troubled as you will be grounded in spirit and on a course to fulfill the plan and purpose for your life and its journey. This has been revealed as you no longer depend on sensory living, and are free from its mind-editing and the restrictions that would previously have confined you. In this freedom is also the power of dominion over your own thoughts and actions, as you will not be influenced by others and their mirroring of life experiences and those limitations. As you will not be a part of this quantum paradigm, you will be less susceptible to be a victim to the fear-based media and the control or limitations of time. This will lead to faith, openness, greater peace, and an eternal purpose. You will not be an independent participant in life, but in unity with the God that created you. Your greater awareness has become the consciousness that no longer keeps you the prisoner of your mind. The mind that had previously held you in limitation as you had taken on that as being your reality, has paved the way for a glorious spiritual journey. You have opened the jail cell of the mind as you have become aware that you have been using all your abilities to sabotage and restrict yourself. You can now experience all that has, is, and will be as you rest in magisterial stillness. You dance in harmony with all creation, creating a cosmic ripple and sound that, in totality, breathes as one in unity.

It's been a blessing to go on this part of the trail with you, and I wish you a life greater than you can imagine. Live each day as your last and be open to learn as if the first.

Blessings,

Reverend Nicholas

About the Author

Nicholas Barrett, renowned performance coach/nutritionist and psychologist, is also an author and speaker specializing in the areas of human development.

His books include *Mind Set to Fitness* and *Get out Of Mind Jail.* The former was inspired from his passion to make people's lives better through his experiences working with countless clients over 17 years in his health and nutrition business. He has always found joy in empowering his clients in their journeys, as watching them succeed taught him that reaching a destination always marks the start of another journey.

It is out of his life experiences that he has become aware that life can be much like an onion in that the deeper we go, the more layers we discover about ourselves and the more we become renewed by this knowledge. Within this concept he continues on a spiritual journey and strives to be the best version of himself with each new day. In using his passion in the study of human psychology, together with his life experiences and wisdom gained, he has written *Get out Of*

Mind Jail. He feels fortunate to be able to empower and assist people not only with their extrinsic level of wellness, but also with their intrinsic well-being. It is indeed this intrinsic component that is most important for realizing our own potential.

Life has blessed each one of us with unlimited potential, yet without the right tuning of the mind, this potential can be likened to a car with a powerful engine, but no suspension to keep it on the road. This can translate to a confused perspective on progress with us going faster and faster in a circle, while all along we would make more progress going slower in a straight line.

Rev. Nicholas feels the tragedy is not that we die, but that we take so long to start living. Our experiences leave an imprint from the moment we leave the womb and begin listening to the words of our parents, classmates, and the media, who too often offer us disappointment, heartbreak, and letdown, which we then edit in our own personal "mind-box" that leaves us in a perpetual state of looking at the present through the mirror of the past, our "mind-jail." He refers to this as the "Human Mind TiVo," where the "mind- jail of presumptive thinking" lives.

After losing both his parents tragically in close succession, Rev. Nicholas has gone forward with even greater strength and faith, dedicating his life to helping others on their walk. Whether through the medium of writing books, leading in church community, or public speaking, his passion is relentless and love for others unending.

He doesn't expect to change human nature with what he does, though he does hope to lift the consciousness of those whom he reaches, offering them the reasoning behind why they think the way that they do, while also guiding them with step-by-step techniques for changing their patterns and habits. These techniques changed his own life into something far bigger and eternal, as his daily self became light, joyous, and refreshed, one that looks forward to each new day with zest, as opposed to struggle, which he used to have when getting up every morning.

Rev. Nicholas wants the best for your life, too, as I am certain you do.

It is his desire and purpose to deliver a unique and powerful message that will be life-changing and empowering to all ages and ethnicities. He is excited at the prospect of what the coming years hold in both his work as an author and public speaker, and following the Master Plan for his life.

His mission: to empower and inspire the human spirit one person at a time using his unique gifts and talents, together with his life experiences to help improve the quality of peoples' daily lives. In his varied roles as author, speaker, church group leader, and nutritionist, it is Rev. Nicholas's goal to help the many who are struggling within their circumstances. His work will never be done, as the need is endless.

Rev. Nicholas can deliver his content publicly or privately.